I0124425

Healing in Action

Healing in Action

Adventure-Based Counseling with Therapy Groups

Barney Straus

ROWMAN & LITTLEFIELD
Lanham • Boulder • New York • London

Published by Rowman & Littlefield
An imprint of The Rowman & Littlefield Publishing Group, Inc.
4501 Forbes Boulevard, Suite 200, Lanham, Maryland 20706
www.rowman.com

Unit A, Whitacre Mews, 26-34 Stannary Street, London SE11 4AB

Copyright © 2018 by The Rowman & Littlefield Publishing Group, Inc.

All rights reserved. No part of this book may be reproduced in any form or by any electronic or mechanical means, including information storage and retrieval systems, without written permission from the publisher, except by a reviewer who may quote passages in a review.

British Library Cataloguing in Publication Information Available

Library of Congress Cataloging-in-Publication Data

Name: Straus, Barney, 1962–, author.
Title: Healing in action : adventure-based counseling with therapy groups / Barney Straus.
Description: Lanham : Rowman & Littlefield, [2018] | Includes bibliographical references and index.
Identifiers: LCCN 2018016763 (print) | LCCN 2018017196 (ebook) | ISBN 9781538117507 (electronic) | ISBN 9781538117484 (hardcover : alk. paper) | ISBN 9781538117491 (pbk. : alk. paper)
Subjects: | MESH: Psychotherapy, Group—methods | Recreation Therapy—methods | Mental Healing—psychology
Classification: LCC RC489.R4 (ebook) | LCC RC489.R4 (print) | NLM WM 430 | DDC 616.89/1653—dc23
LC record available at https://lccn.loc.gov/2018016763

∞ ™ The paper used in this publication meets the minimum requirements of American National Standard for Information Sciences Permanence of Paper for Printed Library Materials, ANSI/NISO Z39.48-1992.

Printed in the United States of America

Contents

Preface   vii

Acknowledgments   xi

Introduction   xiii

Part I: Theoretical Basis and Practical Application of ABC   1

1   Group Theory Applied to ABC   3

2   ABC for Trauma Survivors   13

3   Unique Attributes of ABC   23

Part II: ABC in Outpatient Mental Health Settings   33

4   Overview of a Session   35

5   "Can" Day: Discovering New Abilities within You   39

6   Noodle Day: Using Your Noodle for Positive Change and Growth   45

7   Ball Day: So Long, Gym Class; Hello, Self-Acceptance   57

8   Word Day: Saying and Playing What You Mean   65

9   Paper Day: Beyond Reading and Writing on Paper   75

10   Numbers Day: Multiply Your Strengths   83

11   Rope Day: Securing Success   91

12   Playing-Card Day: Everyone Wins   99

13   Tarp Day: An Indoor Adventure   105

14   No Prop Day: Pure Fun—Willingness Not Included   113

15   Animal Day: Let Your Essence Shine   125

16   Balloon Day: Finding the Levity within You   135

Part III: Adventure-Based Counseling for Recovery from Addiction   141

17 Walking the Walk: ABC and Recovery from Addiction   143

18 Recovery Adventure Day   149

Appendix: Resources   193

References   195

Index   199

About the Author   201

Preface

Healing in Action is the first book to combine current research on group psychotherapy and adventure-based therapy into an easy-to-use, practical guide for therapists working in a variety of settings who would like to expand their use of active methods. It also makes for a great introduction to adventure-based practice and theory for graduate students working toward mental health degrees. The book contains more than a dozen sequences of activities that are designed to be accessible to traditionally trained therapists and engaging and fun for participants. Widely recognized approaches to treatment such as Cognitive Behavioral Therapy (CBT) can enhance the therapeutic impact of these activities.

Since I work primarily in Chicago, where wilderness is scarce, I have focused primarily on a form of adventure therapy known as Adventure-Based Counseling (ABC). ABC incorporates many of the principles of wilderness therapy and challenge course activities so they can be realized within the context of more traditional office-based therapeutic settings. I have worked with older adults in a day-treatment psychosocial rehabilitation program, and I will forever recall with delight seeing these patients, who have contended with chronic mental illness, gleefully playing Moon Ball (described in chapter 7) or Balloon Floor Hockey (described in chapter 16). I have worked with adults and adolescents recovering from addiction who, by realizing experientially that they are able to have sober fun, have found a key to long-term sobriety though ABC. I have worked with adolescents and adults of all ages at an intensive outpatient general mental health program, helping them playfully integrate the central tenets of CBT and Dialectical Behavioral Therapy (DBT) with adventure-based activities. In all of these settings, I have used ABC to bring a sense of novelty, positive risk-taking, and shared fun to the therapeutic process.

I hope to share here some of what I have discovered using adventure activities with a range of populations at different stages of life and in a variety of settings. *Healing in Action* is a guide for therapists who would like to expand their repertoire of approaches to working with groups. The activities described here are designed to be accessible to clinicians with little formal training in adventure education or ABC but who would like to try using creative treatment interventions. It may also offer some new ideas to those already seasoned in Adventure Therapy and/or experiential education. Therapists will be able to use these activities to help their patients experience in vivo the joy, freedom, and playfulness that are the hallmarks of sound mental health.

This book is divided into three sections. Part I offers a theoretical basis for the descriptive material in parts II and III. The first chapter introduces several key theoretical concepts as applied to the use of ABC in groups, including Yalom and Leszcz's (2005) therapeutic factors of group therapy and other unique attributes of groups. Chapter 2 explores how ABC complements trauma-informed approaches to treatment by giving trauma survivors the opportunity to find shared success through adventurous play. Chapter 3 examines some issues related to the unique attributes of ABC, and this content is intended to help more traditionally trained therapists get the maximum benefit from using adventure-based methods. I offer clinical vignettes throughout this first part as a way to bridge the theory of ABC with its practice.

Each of the twelve activity-based chapters in part II describes a session of activities based on a particular theme or material used. They are designed to fill a one-hour block within a treatment program and are especially well suited to intensive outpatient, partial hospitalization, and residential treatment settings. The title of each chapter indicates that session's theme and materials used. For example, chapter 5, "'Can' Day," offers a sequence of activities that can be done using tin cans, and chapter 6, "Noodle Day," offers activities that employ foam pool noodles in various ways. The unifying elements of each chapter are designed in part to simplify the process of gathering supplies. The chapter subtitles often suggest the therapeutic intent. For example, the subtitle of the Noodle Day chapter is "Using Your Noodle for Positive Change and Growth," and the subtitle of the 'Can' Day chapter is "Discovering New Abilities within You." These subtitles hint at a strengths-based approach to treatment. Every activity includes "processing points," which are intended to thoughtfully integrate all the fun being had into group members' treatment goals.

Part III looks more closely at the specific ways in which ABC can help treat addictive disorders. Chapter 17 offers an overview of current research in addictions treatment as well as a historical perspective on how ABC has been used to complement treatment for recovery from addition. Chapter 18 describes a daylong program called Recovery Adventure Day (RAD), which is designed to emphasize the core principles of recovery such as asking for and accepting help and being honest with oneself and others. Clinical vignettes and descriptive photographs are used throughout the text to help bring the activities to life.

Engaging in enjoyable activities offers the immediate reward of experiencing oneself laughing and playing with others; it also functions as a metaphor for challenging situations in life and provides intentional approaches to problem-solving. Using adventure-based activities and interactive games can itself be highly therapeutic, and the structured challenges presented in this book can indirectly reflect on and address the issues that brought patients into treatment. Whether you work in an agency, a hospital, or a private practice setting or are a graduate student preparing to enter a helping profession, you will find ways to bring a sense of novelty, fun, and adventure to your work by using the activities described in this book.

Acknowledgments

Although this book bears my name as its author, the content represents the work of many people. I would like to acknowledge some of them here. First, there are two people without whom this book would not have been possible, Chris Cavert and Christy Nowicki. I am very fortunate to have attended numerous workshops with Chris during his tenure at Northeastern Illinois University, as well as at national conferences. His live workshops and his many books on experiential education have genuinely inspired me. Chris has also been tremendously supportive of my work. He read and critiqued an early draft of the book, and he made useful suggestions throughout. As will quickly become evident, I have borrowed heavily from his significant contributions to the field in selecting activities for this book. Thank you, Chris, for your generosity of time and spirit!

I am also very grateful for the excellent editing work of Christy Nowicki. Christy pushed me to deepen my thinking in the theoretical portions of the book, and she helped me be clear in explaining the activities. Her sharp critical thinking abilities combined with her excellent writing skills made her the perfect editor. I am fortunate to have found her at the right time! Thank you, Christy, for all your hard work on this project.

As I make clear in the text, I believe that a group is much stronger than the sum of its parts. To be fair, this book has taken a group to produce. (I took the advice Gary Kaben offered during his book-writing workshop, to share my material early in the process.) I have asked a number of colleagues to review and comment on various chapters of the book. I would like to thank Ann Bergart, Michael Gass, Seth Harkins, Dannielle Kennedy, Erin McShane, Marcia Nickow, Mo Sook Park, and Jeffrey Roth for their time and interest in my work. I would especially like to thank Shelley Korshak and Emily Olsen for their many contributions to part III. I would also like to thank those adventure-based practitioners who allowed me to interview them about their work. These include Jessica Beaulieu, Deana Grall, Emily Mattimoe, Christine Nicholson, and Meghan O'Donnell.

I would like to acknowledge some of the pioneers of experiential education and Adventure-Based Counseling from whom I have learned so much. In addition to Chris Cavert, mentioned above, I have learned a great deal from Karl Rohnke, another prolific author and creator of group games. Karl has brought joy and excitement to many, and those are qualities I hope to infuse Adventure-Based Counseling with. I am grateful to have been inspired by many people I have met through the Association for Experiential Education, especially those in the Therapeutic Adventure Professionals Group. I would especially like to thank Michael Gass and John Conway for their encouragement and inspiration along the way. Thanks also to my many colleagues at the American Group Psychotherapy Association and the International Association for Social Workers with Groups who have supported my work integrating active methods with interpersonal group therapy.

Thank you to my students at Loyola University Chicago, School of Social Work, and Roosevelt University, Department of Psychology. Many of you have participated in ABC workshops with me, as the photos in this book attest to. Thanks also for your constructive thoughts, as I asked some of you to critique chapters of the book. Thanks to Joel B. for your help with the title.

I would like to add a special note of gratitude for the many professionals and group members who have authorized my adventure-based work through their collaboration and participation. It wouldn't be possible without you!

Thanks to Ben Silverman for his fine photography. And thank you to all the people at Rowman & Littlefield who believed in this project and then helped bring it to life.

Thanks also to my son, Graham, and his friend Sam for posing for a couple of photos. Thank you to my wife, Nancy, for her continual support during the many hours I have spent developing my craft and then writing about it. She also helped with some editing. I truly could not have done any of it without her love and support. Thank you, Nancy!

Introduction

Frank Zappa once asked whether humor belonged in music. His question was a good one, and I think musicians continue to struggle with writing and playing funny music. I can't think of many funny tunes, can you? There are amusing cartoons with musical backgrounds, and funny lyrics can certainly be found (think of Gilbert and Sullivan, Monty Python, etc.), but it's hard to think of music that is funny on its own. This book addresses a similarly perplexing question: Does fun belong in psychotherapy? I argue that it does!

Sigmund Freud suggested that sound mental health was evidenced by the ability to work and love. I think he omitted an important third criterion: the ability to *play*. In recent years, many have written about the therapeutic value of play, including Birk and Tom, Caldwell, and Brown. Some focus more specifically on the beneficial neurological impact of playfulness and laughter (Minden and Marci et al.). Most books about play therapy, such as Stagnitti and Cooper, target children. Eig conceptualizes verbal sparring as a form of rough-and-tumble play for adults. I think of Adventure-Based Counseling (ABC) as physically active play therapy for people of all ages.

Gass, Gillis, and Russell (2012), among the foremost authorities on ABC, define Adventure Therapy (AT) as "the prescriptive use of adventure experiences provided by mental health professionals, often conducted in natural settings, that kinesthetically engage clients on cognitive, affective, and behavioral levels." AT has traditionally been offered in differing lengths and contexts, ranging from several hours to six months or more in the wilderness. This book focuses on a briefer type of adventure therapy known as Adventure-Based Counseling. Specifically, ABC consists of using problem-solving activities with small groups during a bounded and relatively brief period of time. Such programming typically occurs weekly during a course of residential or intensive outpatient treatment. It can also be effectively used in longer-term, open-ended outpatient therapy groups. ABC has been used for decades in the addiction treatment community (Gass & McPhee, 1990; Fletcher, 2013) and it continues to be widely employed in a variety of settings today.

> I was working with a long-term group in which each of the members was so preoccupied with their own problems that it was difficult for them to be attentive to each other's needs. I presented the group with a problem-solving challenge as a way to explore their working relationships with each other. After struggling for some time without making much progress, one of the group members remarked, "We suck." This overt expression of the group members' difficulty collaborating proved useful in helping them become better listeners during the process group sessions. This led to a more committed approach to mutual aid in the therapy group.

Since ABC is more active than most treatment modalities, it offers participants an opportunity to experientially track their progress. When ABC is working at its best, it provides an immediate experience of emotional freedom as well as an illustration or reflection of outside challenges. As patients begin to experience themselves engaging more freely with their fellow group members, they come to realize that their newfound emotional freedom is available in other areas of their lives too. In other words, participants in ABC have ample opportunities to make connections between the way they behave during problem-solving challenges and the way they behave at work, in school, or in their social and familial relationships.

A BIT ABOUT ME

Being a participant in adventure-based activities and group games has been an important part of my own personal development and has impacted many areas of my life. Games were an important part of my life from early on. My happiest childhood memories are of playing large group games such as Capture the Flag and Tug of War. I also enjoyed lighthearted picnic games like three-legged races and the Water Balloon Toss. I felt joy in being part of a force that was much bigger than any one person. I felt that my efforts during those games were valued and appreciated rather than scrutinized, and I delighted in those moments. The outcome of those events seemed much less important than the experience of being part of a shared endeavor. Having active, shared fun, especially outdoors, remains one of my favorite pastimes.

When I was a teenager, my mother sent me on an Outward Bound expedition off the coast of Maine. Though the Outward Bound experience was presented to me as recreational, it had a profound impact on me. I don't know to what extent my mother realized that she was sending me on a therapeutic journey, but it certainly was the most therapeutic experience I had ever engaged in, and it remains so, even after many hours of individual and group therapy, plus regular attendance at self-help group meetings. Surviving on my own for three days on Otter Island was transformative. I was the sole inhabitant on the Island; it rained hard on the final night there, and since the island had just low-lying shrubs, I couldn't make much use out of the plastic tarp and rope I had been provided, and I got soaked. The experience made me appreciate the warm bedroom that my parents had always provided for me. Later, climbing up what seemed like 60 feet of vertical granite using something called a French Ladder made me realize that I could surpass my preconceived limitations. That experience resonates at this very moment, as I sit here writing words that I hope will eventually amount to a book. The "I can't do it" I sometimes feel is very much the same thing I felt when I was halfway up that sheet of granite. The staff at Outward Bound let me dangle on belay for what seemed like a very long time. But unlike the physical fitness tests I endured during grammar school when I would drop off the pull-up bar without having done a single pull-up, the staff at Outward Bound gave me the time and encouragement I needed to find the strength to continue my journey upward. The journey I embarked on during my time at Outward Bound was life-changing.

After discovering in graduate school that there was a long-standing tradition of using outdoor adventure activities and interactive games therapeutically, I became curious to learn more about the therapeutic use of these methods. I attended a Teachers of Experiential and Adventure Modalities (TEAM) Conference at Northeastern Illinois University in Chicago. While at the conference, I participated in a workshop led by Karl Rhonke, a pioneer of problem-solving activities and group games. I was enthralled and delighted by the amount of fun I had! I felt myself smiling for the better part of 90 minutes. Rhonke's gleeful demeanor and slightly devious approach created just the right mix of excitement and silliness to keep the participants engaged and willing to attempt new challenges. I decided at that moment that I wanted to integrate enjoyable experiential methods into my clinical practice. I have been using active methods throughout my career in a variety of clinical settings. I hope to share descriptions of activities and clinical examples of what has worked best in my experience.

A BRIEF HISTORY OF ABC

The roots of ABC can be traced back to the 1800s when summer camps such as those sponsored by the YMCA focused largely on character development. The first intentionally therapeutic camp was established in the 1930s (Gass et al., 2012). Soon after, the Boy Scouts of America brought a military model to the camping culture. The teaching of Native American skills and rituals was involved as well (Gass et al., 2012). The Dallas Salesmanship Club Camp was the first camp to employ mental health therapists. Whether geared to typical children or those with emotional issues, engaging in new challenges to discover new abilities and encourage character development was a hallmark of these summer camps (Gass et al., 2012).

Using interactive games therapeutically also has roots in improvisational theater. In the early part of the 20th century, Viola Spolin and Neva Boyd saw communal play as being essential to the psychological and emotional well-being of the immigrant children they worked with at Hull House, a well-known settlement house in Chicago (Wasson, 2017). They were successful at getting children from diverse backgrounds to engage in playful endeavors together through the use of improvisational games and activities. The children who participated in these challenging events enjoyed enhanced self-expression and heightened self-esteem (Wasson, 2017). Since then, the use of activities with therapeutic groups has gained a great deal of support in the helping professions, especially among social workers (Middleman, 1980). Wright (2005) notes that activities have been used with therapeutic groups to stimulate feelings and discussion, facilitate problem-solving and skill mastery, and build enhanced self-esteem among participants.

An emphasis on character development and trying new things was also central to Outward Bound, an important program brought to the United States by Kurt Hahn, a German educator critical of what he perceived as "social diseases" such as sloth and entitlement among privileged adolescents in the early 20th century. To address these deficits, he created programming focused on a variety of goals including developing skills in athletic abilities, embarking on expeditions, skillfully completing projects and chores, and performing rescue service (Gass et al., 2012; Schoel & Maizell, 2002). Political forces in Germany brought Hahn first to England and later to the United States, where he founded Outward Bound USA in 1962. A rigorous three-week model was developed that included a multi-day "solo" during which participants were given an opportunity to survive on their own in the wild for several days with minimal oversight. Over many years, Outward Bound programming expanded to address the needs of adjudicated youth with limited resources. It soon became clear that such experiential programs had therapeutic value far greater than Hahn's initial intent. Since then, Outward Bound USA has inspired many therapeutic schools and substance abuse treatment programs (Gass et al., 2012).

While private and government funding made Outward Bound accessible to an increasingly wide audience, the length and rigor of the programs limited the number of participants. Recognizing that many more people could benefit from experientially oriented, growth-promoting opportunities, Jerry Pieh founded Project Adventure in 1971. Pieh coined the phrase "adventure-based counseling" and set out to bring a variety of games and problem-solving challenges to schools and hospitals (Gass et al., 2012). Project Adventure offered daylong and even partial-day programs as opposed to the long-term models developed by summer camps and Outward Bound. By 1974, Addison Gilbert Hospital in New England had established a weekly two-hour adventure group (Schoel, Prouty, & Radcliffe, 1988).

Pieh and his colleagues soon realized that the core outcomes of improved self-concept and relational skills were useful to people in all walks of life—not just those with diagnosable mental health issues. The same activities that can be used with therapeutic intentions could also be used with general populations to increase insight about oneself and mutual understanding between participants. Such models integrating lived experience and intellectual exercise owe much to the early 20th-century work of John Dewey, a proponent of bringing experiential methods into the classroom (Dewey, 1938). By 1989, Project Adventure had influenced and developed programming in over 100 treatment centers, even expanding its offerings to include corporate groups and colleges. Project Adventure's training in ABC continues to this day and they offer multi-day workshops in ABC and experiential education throughout the year (Gass et al., 2012; www.pa.org).

The 1980s and 1990s saw an explosion of therapeutic programs and schools influenced by Project Adventure. Many treatment centers had their own challenge courses on site. A challenge course, or "ropes course," typically consists of a series of permanent obstacles or problem-solving challenges in an outdoor setting. The number of treatment centers with on-site challenge courses has decreased in more recent years due to liability issues. While Outward Bound and Project Adventure have good safety records overall, other providers were reckless in their treatment of participants, and preventable deaths and injuries negatively impacted the field (Gass et al., 2012). However, used judiciously and with careful attention to safety, AT and ABC remain highly effective experiential therapeutic modalities that can be combined with more traditional approaches to create a powerful holistic model.

ABC AND GROUP THERAPY

While ABC can be conducted in individual settings (Lung, Stauffer, & Alverez, 2008), it is almost always conducted in the context of a group. ABC works well with therapy groups, and it is best suited to small groups of eight to 14 people. While adventure-based counseling is optimally suited to time-limited groups, it can also be effectively incorporated into longer-term groups. For example, ABC activities can be introduced into a long-term group to address issues such as role lock, in which one or more group members are stuck in a particular dysfunctional role. The adventure therapist can use an activity to highlight such a dynamic so that it can be openly discussed, or the therapist can interrupt it by assigning tasks to members that are not consistent with the role they have been confined to in the group. For example, a group member or family member who seems to be the recipient of much of the group's criticism might be given an opportunity to be the main provider of support and guidance for others through being assigned a leadership role during an activity.

ABC provides ample opportunities for self-reflection, a core tenet of most forms of psychotherapy. The physically involving nature of ABC means that the adventure-based therapist is provided with many opportunities to build what Goldstein and Seigel (2013) describe as "bottom-up awareness," whereby lived experience is integrated into awareness through thoughtful reflection. The guided meaning-making that goes on between therapists and participants engaged in active methods is similar to that which is transacted through more widely accepted methods such as CBT. This may be particularly important as third-party entities such as insurance companies and certification boards want to see treatment goals that are reflective of methods with substantial evidential support. Chapter 3 discusses specific CBT- and DBT-oriented treatment goals that can be realized through the methods described in this text. These goals can be used for treatment planning and reporting, and they accurately reflect both important desired outcomes and the essence of adventure-oriented techniques.

ABC can be an important part of shifting the story people tell both *to* themselves and *about* themselves. By consistently engaging with others in playfully challenging endeavors, patients can change their autobiographies from "I'm a loser who never has any fun because I'm depressed, anxious, and/or addicted" to "I'm somebody who is able to have a good time without hurting myself or anyone else, despite my diagnosis."

Part I

Theoretical Basis and Practical Application of ABC

Chapter One

Group Theory Applied to ABC

Hayden and Molenkamp (2004) define a group as a cluster of individuals who come together to achieve a goal that no one of them could achieve alone. Sports teams, companies, and performing troupes readily come to mind as examples; therapeutic groups, including ABC–based groups, also meet these criteria. As will become clear throughout this chapter, groups are uniquely positioned to help individuals meet their therapeutic goals.

Groups can harness their collective energy to harm or to heal, and the healing that takes place in therapeutic groups can be especially powerful thanks to the complex interpersonal dynamics at play in these settings. We are often able to do jointly what we would not have the courage or ability accomplish alone. Alcoholics Anonymous (AA) and other therapeutic groups empower people to make and sustain changes that they wouldn't be able to without such support. Charles Duhigg (2012) captures the importance of social support in helping people sustain changes when he writes that change becomes real when we see it in other people's eyes. In writing about navigating her grief after having lost her husband at a young age, Cheryl Sandberg (2017) attests to how important groups have been in helping her build resilience through shared efforts that not only strengthen each party individually but result in communities that can overcome adversity together. Groups are powerful!

LEVELS OF FOCUS

Short and McRae (2010) identify several levels of focus to consider when thinking about group dynamics The first level of focus looks at individual group members: their personality traits, talents, physical attributes, personal tastes, and so forth. As will become clear throughout the vignettes and when you begin to use activities with your groups, seeing people in action readily reveals how they function more generally. For example, ABC can be used to unearth individuals' propensities to assume particular roles in groups. The second level of focus addresses relational dynamics such as attraction, affection, and competition. These interpersonal dynamics can be explored through structured activities, though they may be given closer attention during discussion-based process group sessions. The third level of focus is the group-as-a-whole (GAAW), and it considers that specific individuals act not only in their own self-interest, but also *on behalf of the entire group*. The GAAW lens recognizes that as social beings, we are strongly influenced by the collective, and the GAAW energy is integral to the power of ABC as participants experience themselves joining with others in meaningful ways. Kurland and Salmon (1992) concur that the use of activities helps the group worker focus on the group as a whole. Individual and GAAW frames will be used throughout the theoretical material in part I to support the ways in which ABC is uniquely therapeutic.

THE INTENTIONAL USE OF METAPHOR

It is imperative that adventure-based therapists help their group members extract meaning from their experience in ABC. While being engaged in a collective endeavor is in and of itself therapeutic, we want to make sure to provide opportunities for participants to apply their experience to other areas of their lives. This is often accomplished through the therapeutic use of metaphor. Gass et al. (2012) and Schoel and Maizell (2002) have each described several types of metaphors that can be effectively used during ABC programming. In each case, metaphorical application offers opportunities for participants to use what they learn from engaging in relatively simple tasks in a controlled setting to enhance their capacity to cope with life's many day-to-day challenges.

The therapeutic impact of activities can be heightened through the use of what Gass et al. (2012) refer to as "structured metaphors" and what Schoel and Maizell (2002) call "directed metaphors." These "frontloaded" ideas are suggested by the therapist before participants engage in an activity (Itan, 1998). For example, before beginning the Mousetraps activity described in chapter 15, participants are invited to think about what emotional "traps" they need to avoid stepping into in their relationships. An example of an emotional trap might be getting into an argument with a feisty relative, or feeling responsible for another person's moods. During the activity, a participant is verbally guided through a field of live mousetraps while blindfolded. Through the use of structured and co-created metaphor, the mousetraps come to represent other sticky situations that the participant would like to avoid stepping into.

After having crossed the field of traps, the participant might be asked how they felt about having received the support from their guide, and how this might be similar to how they experience support in other areas of their lives. This type of metaphor, suggested after the completion of an activity, is referred to as an "analogous metaphor" by Gass et al. (2012) and as a "co-created metaphor" by Schoel and Maizell (2002).

In this example, two types of metaphors (structured/directed before the activity and analogous/co-created both before and afterward) are used to highlight potentially meaningful issues for the participant. In thinking about what the traps represent, participants are guided to consider and name those things that have proven dangerous to them. The presence of the traps brings the potential of future danger into the present moment. The potential danger of getting ensnared in a mousetrap feels real in the moment and may make it easier for the participant to imagine that the dangers being discussed are likewise real and immediate, especially if the person doesn't get sufficient support—that's where analogous metaphorical application comes into play. Staying closely connected to a guide during the activity can easily be made analogous to staying closely connected to one's sponsor, therapist, or other support person.

The last type of metaphor is known as "spontaneous" (Gass et al., 2012) or "open" (Schoel & Maizell, 2002). Rather than being prompted by the therapist, such a metaphor may occur to a participant as a natural outcome of their involvement in the group. For example, let's say a participant has a tendency to be controlling. In the Mousetraps example, a guide might come to realize that they are micro-managing during the exercise, that they have gone beyond the parameters of offering compassionate support to the point at which they do not trust their partner to follow their directions. Having had such an epiphany, the participant can reflect on the ways in which this quality may interfere with their experience in other contexts. For example, this person might come to realize that they have been similarly controlling with their college-age child and that becoming more trusting might enhance their relationship with the emerging adult in their life.

The questions that group members must ask themselves in order to solve the various challenges while participating in ABC can be readily applied to other areas of their lives. The main task for the therapist employing ABC is to help the participants transfer their experience during the activity to outside contexts. This transfer of learning is very similar to skills employed by therapists using other structured approaches such as CBT and DBT. ABC achieves similar outcomes though the application of metaphor and through direct action, as opposed to through the filling out of familiar worksheets, during which change can remain an idea, as opposed to a realized behavior.

STAGES OF GROUP DEVELOPMENT

A metaphor that is commonly applied to all types of therapeutic groups has to do with a group's life cycle. Much has been written about how groups move through a progression of life stages similar to that of all living entities—ranging from their infancy or beginnings to their eventual demise at termination. From this general structure, a variety of models have been developed to expand upon this idea. Garland, Jones, and Kolodny (1965) construct a five-stage model that includes a competitive phase as a precursor to a more productive working phase. Schiller (1997) argues that this construction does not apply to groups of women or other disempowered groups. She says that such populations require a period of building trust and mutuality before they can engage in any conflict. She goes on to describe constructive conflict in groups as a period of "challenge and change," a more positive view of conflict than the jockeying for power and control that Garland, Jones, and Kolodny (1965) describe. Yalom and Leszcz (2005) and others (Rutan, Stone, & Shay, 2007) propose other models. Nevertheless, all theories of linear group development agree that groups have an introductory beginning stage, a working middle stage that constitutes the bulk of the group's productive time, and an ending period during which transfer of gains made in the group to other contexts becomes important.

The activities described in this book can be effectively employed during any phase of a group's life. The abundance of activity involved in ABC tends to move groups through the stages of development somewhat quickly, which is one of the reasons why ABC is especially well-suited to time-limited groups. The ice-breakers and more playful activities are conducive to the tasks of the early stages of a group. The problem-solving and trust-building activities (the majority of what appears in this book) are useful during the working period of a group's life. The intentional use of metaphor, discussed above, is useful during the later stages of a group as it is what helps group members meaningfully apply their experience in the group to their lives. Note that through using ABC, a group can move through all three phases in a single session, or over a longer period of time when working with longer-term or open-ended groups. I go into greater detail in chapter 4 regarding the rationale for intentionally sequencing activities.

Yalom and Leszcz (2005) refer to structured activities such as those used in ABC as "accelerating techniques," meaning that they help propel groups through the developmental stages faster than typically occurs through talking alone. This can be both beneficial and a drawback, depending on the overall goals of the group. One criticism that Yalom and Leszcz make is that the accelerative impact of ABC may come at the expense of a more organic developmental process. Given the time constraints that many people and programs face, the advantages of moving a group more expediently into a working phase may outweigh any potential drawbacks of using ABC. Only long-term interpersonal process groups have the luxury of allowing a more natural developmental process. It follows that ABC is especially well-suited to time-limited groups and groups in which membership changes frequently such as in residential treatment centers and intensive outpatient programs (IOP) and partial hospitalization programs (PHP), where patients cycle in and out over a period of weeks or months.

ABC'S INFLUENCE ON THE THERAPEUTIC FACTORS OF GROUPS

Irvin Yalom's research on the therapeutic value of group work, conducted in the 1970s at Stanford University, is some of the most respected to date, particularly his description of the eleven therapeutic factors of group psychotherapy (Yalom, 1995; Yalom & Leszcz, 2005). Many of the therapeutic factors that Yalom and Leszcz document can be activated and enhanced by ABC methods. In the following pages, I describe a few of the therapeutic factors that are especially likely to be activated through the use of shared fun and adventure.

Instillation of Hope is one of the most important therapeutic factors. Very often those coming into treatment feel hopeless. Being able to observe others' successes prompts the thought "If they can do it, so can I." This process can happen simply though observation. Change in most therapeutic groups happens slowly, such as when a group member gradually grows less combative in their interpersonal relationships. But if a group member sees another climb over a 12-foot wall, they immediately come to believe that they too may be capable of doing the same. Group members also receive direct encouragement and an instilled sense of hope from supportive peer relationships they develop in treatment. Instillation of Hope is further accentuated by the "fun factor" of ABC. If patients can experience a sense of pleasurable playfulness during ABC sessions, they are likely to feel hopeful that more of the same awaits. I discuss the therapeutic value of play in greater detail in chapters 2 and 3.

Finally, a sense of renewed hopefulness can result directly from shared success in ABC challenges such as in the successful solving of problems. When I initially present challenges to groups, I sometimes hear someone say, "That's impossible." During one program with people in recovery from addiction, I got such a response when I presented All Touch (chapter 5), and again after introducing Whale Watch (chapter 18). Both tasks were readily completed, so in effect the group went from "That's impossible" to "We just did that!" in a matter of minutes. This experience was easily transferable to group members' struggles with addiction, which at times can feel like a hopeless cause.

Universality is another key therapeutic factor of groups. The feeling that others have the same problems as we do and are open to talking about them and asking for assistance removes a great burden from the minds of many patients who often mistakenly feel that they are alone in their plight. The cliché "Misery loves company" may apply. The beauty here is that people quickly become less miserable once they bond with others through a shared problem-solving endeavor. Universality is enhanced through ABC activities as all group members contend with the same set of challenges.

The African word *Ubuntu* means "Sharing what we have and who we are." High 5 Adventure, a provider of educational adventure programs and related materials, created a product called Ubuntu Cards several years ago. These cards work on the same principle as Spot It cards, which can be found at many bookstores and game shops. Each card contains eight unique images, and every card contains at least one image that is identical to one image on every other card. In other words, every pair of cards has one matching image (I don't tell this to group members at first). In most cases the images are placed in a different part of the card, or are different sizes, so the similarities may not be easily detected at first.

These cards can be used for an icebreaker early in a program. Each group member is given a card, and then is asked to mingle with other group members. Each pair of group members has a dual task—first, find a matching image on their cards, and then find something else about themselves that they have in common. Once they have accomplished both tasks, the pair swaps cards and each finds a different partner to pair and share with. After several rounds, I ask the group members whether anyone was unable to find a matching image with another person. Usually one or two people say that they got stuck at some point. I then explain that every card has at least one matching image with every other card, the idea being that points of connection can always be found if we are willing to be patient and persistent as we look for them. I go on to ask where else in life group members may have experienced difficulty finding points of connection with others (an analogous metaphor). This is a dynamic that many people experience when they first go to a peer-support meeting such as Alcoholics Anonymous (AA). "I'm not nearly as bad as these people," some will say to themselves, while others might balk at differences in educational level or professional status between themselves and others. Newcomers to AA are advised to look for similarities between themselves and others (namely, a desire to stop drinking) rather than the differences. As happens consistently through using ABC, participants experience themselves having overlooked things they have in common with each other. In finding commonalities with those who at first glance seem different from them, a sense of universality is realized. Interpersonal Learning is a therapeutic factor that offers participants an opportunity to learn about themselves by reflecting on their interpersonal relationships. This may surface unconsciously during an ABC program, as might be the case, for example, when a group member is continually directing others while remaining ignorant of their own need to remain in control, a fact another member might point out during a reflective session.

> I was leading an activity called Key Punch (chapter 10) that asks all of the members of a group to make ordered physical contact with a series of numbered spot markers on the ground. One group member was generating very productive ideas for the group. She outlined a way of approaching the task that made sense to others and she described and directed an orderly manner for the group members to touch the spots in rapid succession. During one of the attempts that she had orchestrated, she failed to step on her own numbered spot marker. She took responsibility for this error, and other group members commented that it was refreshing to be working with a leader who was willing to take responsibility for their errors. The emergent leader of the group was receptive to the constructive feedback that was offered by her peers.

Schoel and Maizell (2002) agree that constructive feedback is a critical component of ABC. They note the "Four C's" of such corrective behavior being that it is given in a way that is caring, concrete, concise, and clear. The adventure therapist is advised to provide opportunities for group members to share with each other what behaviors they notice in each other during the activities. This is made immediate by its application to lived, "here and now" behavior, which is easier to see and comment on when physical tasks are introduced.

Altruism is a therapeutic factor that is usually required during ABC programming in order for the group to succeed. Yalom and Leszcz (2005) note that the opportunity to behave altruistically is a unique attribute of group therapy. People tend to feel good about themselves when they provide assistance to others. Altruism can be combined with Imparting of Information, another therapeutic factor, to leave group members feeling that they were helpful to others. For example, more often than not, some members of a group will have a natural facility for spatial analysis and problem-solving strategies (Gardner, 2011). When these individuals become willing to share their knowledge with the rest of the group, the group benefits. Likewise, those providing the knowledge can feel good about having been of assistance. This kind of sharing of information is one type of altruistic act, among many others, that can be enacted through ABC. Altruism is further accentuated through ABC because the activities are designed to encourage mutual support. Altruism is most apparent during activities that require physical support such as trust-building activities and The Wall.

As the name implies, The Wall offers group members an opportunity to boost each other up and over a 10- or 12-foot wood structure using only each other for support. The wall may metaphorically represent personal obstacles for group members that, with enough support, can be overcome. For example, a person who grew up in a family in which they were constantly criticized may have developed low self-confidence that prevents them from applying for desirable jobs. The emotional and physical boost offered by the group on the challenge course can, over time, replace the impact of the original toxic messages delivered by the family.

Imitative Behavior is another therapeutic factor that lends itself especially well to ABC methods. Being engaged in ABC means that participants will be mimicking each other's physical behavior. The idea of lending a helping hand may be inspirational, but actually doing so can be transformative. ABC offers many opportunities for participants to repeat actions that others have found to work well. This process is representative of what occurs over a longer period of time as group members try to emulate each other's successes in terms of their life goals.

Catharsis is a therapeutic factor that often happens by surprise when a group member experiences a strong outpouring of emotion such as sorrow or rage. Such ventilation is often accompanied by personal reflection and revelation. Such an epiphany can allow them to make life-changing decisions. The unique nature of ABC challenges that invite participants out of their comfort zones creates an environment with rich potential for catharsis to occur.

Cathartic moments can be particularly powerful when experienced in conjunction with another therapeutic factor: Existential Factors. This kind of catharsis is especially relevant when using "high ropes" adventure activities (chapter 18). Relying on the support of others, especially when suspended in midair, tends to bring about powerful feelings for participants: "I'm scared, and I feel like I could die, and I realize that I want to live because I really value the people in my life." Very often the realization that life is transient leads them to the conclusion that they would be better off valuing their intimate relationships during their time on the planet. Similarly, The Maze, or No Way Out (chapter 18), frequently leads to cathartic moments for group members as they come to realize, through direct visceral experience, just how resistant they are to receiving help from others. I have had group members tell me that the impact of The Maze has remained with them for weeks and even years afterward. Direct, kinesthetic experience is uniquely impactful.

Yalom and Leszcz (2005) posit that Group Cohesiveness is the most meaningful and important of all therapeutic factors. Group psychotherapy really takes off when group members begin to trust one another enough to take real emotional risks, such as honestly sharing their thoughts and feelings with each other. This is brought about in ABC initially though icebreakers, during which a shared sense of fun emerges, and later though trust-building

Accepting a boost from the group. *Photo by the author.*

challenges, which usually involve working through some fear. We tend to develop positive feelings that make us want to return to groups that are enjoyable. Shared enjoyable experience also builds trust and closeness between group members. The structured nature of ABC results in group members taking physical and emotional risks sooner than they would in groups that exclusively employ talking as the methodology.

I have frequently witnessed cohorts in intensive outpatient treatment settings grow more cohesive following their participation in Recovery Adventure Day, described in chapter 18. The specific nature of an individual's character and symptomatology can influence the degree to which they are amenable to feeling connected to others. Those with severe histories or symptomatology may be challenged in this area. But I have also seen that after having joined as a group more deeply through a day of shared novelty and problem-solving, patients feel as though they really have shared an adventure, and they tend to reminisce about their experience in much the same way that groups who have traveled together revel in their shared memories. This is the definition of Yalom and Leszcz's Group Cohesiveness (2005).

To summarize, ABC can accentuate many of the helpful dynamics of therapeutic groups. The exercises involved tend to amplify and accelerate many of the therapeutic factors mentioned by Yalom and Leszcz (2005). The bonus is that they do so in a way that emphasizes positive risk-taking and having fun, two behaviors that may be especially valuable to members of therapeutic groups.

Many mental health patients have histories that include developmental and acute trauma. Very frequently, developmental trauma (e.g., feeling unloved by one's parents) leads to addictive behavior, which in turn can result in acute trauma, such as being arrested, shot, or raped. Trauma survivors may be uniquely positioned to benefit from ABC. Their traumatic past may have left them feeling frightened of new, novel experiences. Participation in ABC may restore trauma survivors' sense of safety and trust in their peers. The next chapter explores specific ways in which ABC is helpful to this population.

Chapter Two

ABC for Trauma Survivors

In recent years, the impact of trauma has garnered increased attention in the helping professions. Besel van der Kolk (2014) and others (Korshak, Nickow, & Straus, 2013; Dayton, 2007; Mellody, 1989) suggest that the unmet emotional needs of children are often experienced as traumatic and that those who were traumatized by emotional abuse or neglect as children develop an impaired ability to form secure attachments as adults. Such individuals might give up trying to build meaningful relationships (Korshak, Nickow, & Straus, 2013). They are also vulnerable to becoming attached to addictive substances and behaviors rather than to other people (Flores, 2004). Through experiencing a sense of safety in ABC, trauma survivors can become free of old survival strategies and replace them with healthy, adaptive, relationship-building skills and enhanced physiological regulation.

THE THERAPEUTIC BENEFIT OF MOVEMENT

Van der Kolk (2014) posits that the physical body is profoundly impacted by trauma survivors' intense, even single-minded focus on suppressing the inner chaos that results from feeling worthless or unlovable. Chronic diseases such as fibromyalgia, chronic fatigue, constipation, and even basic bodily functions such as sleep regulation and gastrointestinal function are disrupted by the psychological malaise that can stem from trauma. Accordingly, van der Kolk (2014) says that any effective treatment for trauma must address these basic physiological housekeeping functions and restore broken connections between the mind and body. Blech (2009) notes that even small amounts of exercise can make a difference in people's overall health. I agree with both authors and I feel that the physical aspect of ABC is helpful on many levels. ABC can function as mild exercise in that it gets participants moving without making them feel as if they are repeating a routine, as often happens during formal exercise regimens, but they are *moving*, and that is what counts. An ABC program on the more vigorous side may yield the endorphin boost that exercise delivers, but even a less exhilarating program will likely have some physiological benefits.

Additionally, group movement provides an effective way of engaging patients. Van der Kolk (2014) notes that for patients whose life experiences have taught them that shutdown and hyper-defensiveness are the only ways to ensure survival, verbal methods of engaging and processing may be moot. Trauma survivors, he argues, may get more out of simply helping to arrange chairs before a meeting or joining in a percussive jam session than from sitting and recounting their past difficulties. Similarly, when Stuart Brown, medical doctor and founder of the National Institute for Play, senses that his patients are feeling resistant to being playful, he gets them moving as a first step (Brown, 2010). Both examples highlight that emotional connections can be built through shared physical endeavors, and these experiences may trump more verbally centered methods.

Because of the physical harm many trauma survivors have endured, van der Kolk says they need to *kinesthetically* come to understand that they are safe. He claims that only a physiologically corrective experience can counter the long-lasting impact of trauma. Brown (2010) adds that any activity that involves movement fosters learning, flexibility, innovation, and resilience, among other things. Norman Diodge's (2015) findings on neuroplasticity (a process through which new neural pathways are developed) support van der Kolk's and Brown's hypotheses in suggesting that play begets more play by promoting new neural connections that did not previously exist. Play experienced through ABC can lead to increased playfulness in all areas of life.

THE THERAPEUTIC USE OF SEMIPERMEABLE BOUNDARIES

Mellody (1989) posits that developmental trauma is often accompanied by destructive boundaries (i.e., overly intrusive or absentee parenting) that result in survivors becoming preoccupied with the needs of others. Short and McRae (2010) and Roth (2004) comment that overly rigid boundaries in a group or family can lead to feelings of suffocation among individuals, while diffuse boundaries can engender a sense of abandonment. The authors suggest that semipermeable boundaries are conducive to learning and growth in most groups and may be particularly important in groups of trauma survivors.

Schoel and Maizell (2002) suggest that adventure-based therapists can break the cycle of trauma by providing functional, semipermeable boundaries through using carefully structured activities by which participants can experience a renewed sense of personal efficacy and freedom of choice. Facilitators will often define physical boundaries and specific, tangible goals as part of ABC programming.

> All Cross is an activity that offers a good illustration of how an ABC activity can be used to foster a healthy balance between secure boundaries and personal autonomy. In All Cross, group members stand in a circle with a spot marker in the middle. They are asked to swap places with their counterpart across the circle from them in the fastest time possible, with the following parameters: each person must make contact with the spot in the middle while avoiding making contact with any other member of the group. These instructions are often followed with a series of questions from members of the group. I usually reply that provided they stick to the two main guidelines, they can do whatever they wish. By making such a statement, I have set functional, semipermeable boundaries—the central message being that there is room for creativity and innovation within specific parameters.

Very often group members get so focused on the movement pattern during All Cross that they lose track of the secondary detail that each person must make contact with the spot in the middle. The group is often surprised when I inform them that the second detail got overlooked. This dynamic is highly transferable to other contexts though the use of analogous metaphor. For example, in work settings, a deal is signed, but various contingencies are overlooked; or think of a person who regularly attends AA meetings but neglects to work the steps of recovery. A group's initial reaction is usually to think about who the culprit was. I tend to allow the group members to decide for themselves whether or not to speak up or remain silent on this point. Again, this decision-making process is transferable to other contexts. When do we decide to "blow the whistle" when we notice a dysfunctional pattern of behavior in a family member, group, or organization? The recent "Me Too" movement represents a collective willingness to call attention to sexual boundary violations in work environments. When do family members decide to mention another family member's self-destructive behavior, and when do they decide to "go along to get along?" By attending to the detail of verifying if the spot marker has been touched by every group member, I have communicated that I am maintaining consistent boundaries for the group within a framework that welcomes creativity and experimentation.

KINESTHETIC AWARENESS AND FOCUSING ON THE PRESENT MOMENT

Van der Kolk (2014) maintains that activities that involve being focused in the present are essential to post-traumatic stress disorder (PTSD) recovery. He claims that being able to perceive visceral sensation is the very foundation of present-oriented emotional awareness. He goes on to say that "physical self-awareness is the first step in repairing the tyranny of the past." The novel materials employed in ABC, as well as familiar materials used in novel ways, offer one path to increased tactile awareness. The pool noodle activities described in chapter 6 are a good example of this. Because the materials are unfamiliar to most participants, especially when used away from water, they tend to increase group members' kinesthetic awareness. People tend to pay special attention to new stimuli. Goldstein and Siegel (2013) posit that enhanced kinesthetic awareness helps to strengthen participants' emotional regulatory skills.

> Gotcha! is an ice-breaker that engenders a sense of playful lightheartedness in group members. With the group members standing in a circle, the leader asks everyone to put their left palm face up in front of them, as if they were carrying a tray. Next, participants should position their right index finger on top of the person's outstretched left hand to their immediate right. At this point, everyone in the circle should have the index finger of the person to their left positioned just over their left palm while at the same time having their own right finger positioned similarly over the palm of the person to their right. On the group leader's cue (One, two, three!), the challenge is for each person to simultaneously try to capture the finger to their left while escaping the grasp of the person's hand to their right. Each person keeps their own score—the maximum points a person can achieve in a round is two—one for escaping and another for capturing. If a group member gets two points, I let that person count off for the following round. For added fun, feel free to switch directions and allow two new people to count off. The sense of anticipation involved in this game tends to heighten group members' sense of the immediate moment.

Though Gotcha! involves some physical contact, it does so in a way that is comfortable for most people. Nevertheless, it is always advisable to make room for participants to talk about the way that the touch is impacting them. This activity encourages mild risk-taking and spontaneity, two important ingredients for the therapeutic journey. Often a group will become more willing to engage in higher-level challenges after they have played Gotcha!

THERAPEUTIC USE OF TOUCH

ABC initiatives that involve physical contact are useful in heightening kinesthetic awareness, but they introduce challenges as well. All too often, the use of touch in our society is limited to aggressive or sexual behavior. Trauma survivors, especially those who have been victims of sexual or physical abuse, face a dilemma: they crave and need healing touch but are often frightened of physical contact.

Though many ABC activities involve physical contact, in some cases the contact is focused and intentional while in other cases it is incidental. Sometimes activities involving incidental contact allow trauma survivors to build

Gotcha! *Photo by Ben Silverman.*

the courage and trust they need to engage in activities in which the contact is more intentional. Schoel and Maizell (2002) suggest that therapists' attention to physical safety during ABC programs may transfer to a sense of emotional safety for participants. Goldstein (2018) suggests that using an object to buffer skin-to-skin contact may allow some participants to become more fully engaged in an activity without becoming overly focused on the contact itself. One example of this is using pool noodles or bandanas to connect people engaged in the Human Knot challenge (chapters 6 and 18). Another might be placing a book or magazine between the hands of two people leaning toward each other.

A young-adult female trauma survivor who was participating in a day-long AT program opted out of an opportunity to be the "willow" in the Willow in the Wind activity, a trust-building exercise in which one person stands in the middle of a tight circle of their peers and allows the other group members to tilt them back and forth around the circle. Having this much physical contact can be overly stimulating for many trauma survivors and may even simulate the out-of-control experience of traumatic events. Later in the day, the individual participated in an initiative called Telephone Pole (TP) Shuffle in which group members are asked to rearrange the order in which they are standing on a telephone pole lying horizontally on the ground. Due to the difficulty maintaining balance while standing on a log, the only way to successfully navigate the task is by accepting physical support from others. Because group

Willow in the Wind. *Photo by the author.*

members are primarily focused on changing positions during this process, they may more easily accept a helping hand. The woman in question stayed engaged during the entirety of TP Shuffle. The last activity of the day was The Wall, during which group members boost each other up and over a tall wall. Obviously, this requires significant physical support. Through her experience feeling safely and securely supported during TP Shuffle, the patient who had opted out of being the willow for Willow in the Wind that morning was able to conquer The Wall later that same day. The metaphorical impediment to this individual's personal growth was not being able to be open with others and to accept their help. The patient had a powerfully healing experience because she kinesthetically came to understand that she was safe, and she was able to make significant gains in her therapeutic goals that day.

THERAPEUTIC USE OF PERCEIVED RISK

Trauma may cause survivors to shut down emotionally in self-protection, hence, they then may only respond to intense stimulation and find more ordinary events to be boring. Trauma survivors frequently seek out activities that are *actually* dangerous, such as skydiving, recreational drug use, or promiscuous sexual behavior, and they report feeling numb in the absence of such intense stimulation. Adventure-based therapists engage participants in

Telephone Pole Shuffle. *Photo by the author.*

activities that involve *perceived risk*, in which the actual risk has been mini-mized, through careful attention to procedures and proper use of equipment, so that the experience provides an immediate antidote to the numbness that plagues some trauma survivors.

At the same time, the thrills generated by the perceived risks associated with adventurous activities provide a safe environment in which to reestab-lish a sense of trust in themselves and others. Activities such as surfing large waves and marathon running are scary at first but become enjoyable as the body adjusts and a new chemical balance is maintained (van der Kolk, 2014). The same process may apply to some ABC activities, which can be initially terrifying but eventually become enjoyable. The experience of being physi-cally safe in spite of perceived risk can be achieved through the use of "trust leans" and other ABC activities that involve "spotting" (one person physical-ly shielding another from potential injury). High Ropes course elements such as the Leap of Faith, pictured below, offer an especially powerful experience of perceived risk.

On the other hand, some trauma survivors may be prone to hypervigi-lance. Individual assessments should be used when deciding which activities to use with which individuals. The lethargic individual may be in a better

Taking a Leap of Faith. *Photo by the author.*

position to assume a high degree of perceived risk than those who are hyper-sensitive to any stimulation. An emphasis on individualized care and support of participants should be maintained. Taken together, these aspects of ABC do much to instill a renewed sense of safety and trust among participants.

ABC can provide opportunities not only to reestablish a sense of physical safety for survivors but also a sense of relational safety. Van der Kolk (2014) notes that if we feel safe and loved, our brains become specialized in exploration, play, and cooperation. If, on the other hand, we felt frightened and unwanted as children, our brains become specialized in feelings of fear and abandonment. I suggest that the reverse may also be true: by engaging freely in joyful play through ABC activities, group members may experience feeling safe and loved. A sense of safety is provided in ABC through the implementation of semipermeable boundaries and proper use of equipment, while love is communicated through mutual care between the therapist and the group, and between group members. If participants can experience feeling loved and safe during ABC sessions, then there is hope that they will be able to experience these emotions in other contexts of their lives.

Perceived risk and an emphasis on kinesthetic awareness are two qualities that distinguish ABC as a therapeutic modality and make it particularly relevant to survivors of trauma. The next chapter explores some other unique facets of ABC and is intended to prepare the traditionally trained therapist to maximize the benefits of incorporating ABC into their work.

Chapter Three

Unique Attributes of ABC

In addition to an emphasis on physical activity and the conscious use of metaphor (both discussed in the preceding chapters), other distinguishing features of ABC include incorporation of the outdoors, an emphasis on playfulness, and a shift in role for the therapist using active methods. These additional unique qualities of ABC are explored in this chapter, along with some practical matters such as training and treatment planning. Taken together, these concepts are meant to provide further guidance for clinicians wanting to incorporate ABC into their practice.

THE THERAPEUTIC USE OF THE OUTDOORS

ABC is often conducted in outdoor settings, which can be therapeutic in and of itself. Some authors observe that as human beings have grown increasingly distant from nature, mental health symptoms have increased (Gass, Gillis, & Russell, 2012; Williams, 2017). Recent research corroborates this hypothesis and also supports a corollary: exposure to nature makes people feel and act better (Williams, 2017). Williams notes that spending time in nature makes us healthier, more creative and empathic, and more apt to engage with others and the world. The author reports that exposure to nature immediately lowers people's anxiety and stress levels. After being in nature, people can think more clearly, and they tend to cheer up. Williams also cites research indicating that walking in a natural setting results in much less time obsessing about negative thoughts than walking in an urban environment. In their discussion of ABC, Gass et al. (2012) note that several writers see exposure to nature as the *primary healing factor* in adventure therapy programming, overshadowing even therapists' interventions. For example, one ABC participant commented that working with a group in the outdoors allowed his mind to wander at times and gave him a sense of personal freedom that being confined by walls and ceilings did not.

Being outdoors in a natural setting has the potential to augment and enhance the therapeutic process. The body is able to absorb vitamin D through exposure to sunlight, for a start. Then, having nothing but the sky overhead evokes the cliché "The sky is the limit." Outdoor environments tacitly create a sense of adventure and of discovering new environments, whether they be physical places or psychological states of mind. Nevertheless, as previously stated, many of the principles embedded in outdoor ABC programs easily transfer to more conventional treatment settings, such as a large group room. The most notable of these is a sense of playfulness.

THE THERAPEUTIC VALUE OF PLAY

As mentioned in the previous chapter, the experience of being involved in play is a hallmark of ABC. Stuart Brown (2010) notes that play is pleasurable as it engages and enlivens us and is an important component of being a fulfilled human being. Unfortunately, many adults confine their play to drinking and talking. ABC offers an opportunity to rekindle playfulness that may have been dormant. Brown claims that the opposite of play is not work but depression; it follows that engaging in play may then lift clients out of depressive episodes. Schoel and Maizell (2002) explain that having fun with others is pleasurable and brings participants into the present moment. Brown (2010) concurs that when we are in a "state of play" we lose the passage of time and experience diminished self-consciousness. Self-consciousness plagues many mental health patients, so this kind of emotional freedom can be uniquely therapeutic.

> I was working with a group of adolescent patients at a day-treatment program. Many of these youngsters were recovering from school refusal that resulted from their feeling like social outcasts. I introduced a game of Pass the Pasta (chapter 6), and we built up to two foam noodles of different colors moving around the circle in opposite directions. There was much laughter as the noodles got passed around. The collective experience of play became more powerful than the experience of any one person. After the commotion had calmed down, one group member said that she felt as though she had been temporarily transported to another place and time—as if her lived reality had temporarily shifted to one in which she felt free to engage fully in the moment. This was a relief from the self-conscious preoccupation that haunted her much of the time, and it was a great transferable lesson that she was more than her school refusal, that her particular issues need not rule her life, and she could still find opportunities to have fun and really live!

The six stages of play (Anticipation, Surprise, Pleasure, Understanding, Strength, and Poise), as defined by the Strong Museum of Play in Rochester,

Pass the Pasta. *Photo by Ben Silverman.*

New York, each relate to the psychotherapeutic process inherent in ABC. I briefly comment on each of these stages in the following paragraphs.

Anticipation, or a sense of uncertainty, is the first stage of play. Uncertainty regarding outcome applies to all competitive games, and a sense of the unknown—of engaging in a novel pursuit—is central to ABC. Part of what makes ABC uniquely effective is this very factor. By participating in ABC, group members are tacitly communicating that they are willing to try something new. This "change mindset" is directly transferable to other therapeutic modalities such as CBT and carries with it a sense of anticipation.

An element of Surprise, stage two, is often present in ABC as a therapist using an activity may modify the guidelines after a group has started to work on it. For example, during the Stepping Stones activity described in chapter 18, participants are often surprised when the facilitator removes one of the group's resources (represented by the platforms) after the group has lost physical contact with it. Group members will sometimes protest, "Hey, that's not fair" or "You didn't say you would actually take it away!" Even if the facilitator did mention this during the instructions, the group members are surprised to actually experience the loss. This experience is designed to remind participants that they need to remain vigilant about remaining connected to their resources at all times. Also, being surprised by experientially reflecting on one's own behavior is what sets ABC apart from other modalities. Whereas during a CBT session a patient will report on their behavior outside the group, during an ABC session, they get to experience the behavior in vivo, and with the support of a group and therapist. This kind of experiential learning often contains an element of surprise.

Stage three, Pleasure, is evident whenever people are laughing together—a frequent occurrence during an ABC session. The shared sense of enjoyment is pervasive and provides an immediate antidote to mood disorders such as anxiety and depression. Also, because ABC is action-based, it emphasizes the behavioral dimension of CBT, and people are likely to experience a sense of pleasure from putting their behavioral treatment plan into action—for example, taking a 30-minute daily walk.

The next stage, Understanding, is integral to effective ABC. Participants' insights are fostered through the metaphorical application of activities to situations in their lives. Of course, many psychotherapeutic processes, including psychoanalysis, accentuate personal insight, but the opportunity to gain insight through real-time experience is especially powerful, salient, and observable. Additionally, ABC methods offer opportunities to reframe the way a person thinks about him- or herself. For example, an individual with a negative self-image due to their weight might experience their body in a new, more positive way in an activity such as Incomplete Bridge (shown on the next page), where the base of a fulcrum must be adequately weighted to support the other group members. A heavy person might experience himself as valuable, strong, and supportive of others during this process.

As mentioned previously, ABC is a strengths-based approach to treatment. Van der Kolk (2014) maintains that a strengths-based approach allows patients to experience a sense of competency. Adventure therapists offer opportunities for their group members to develop a sense of mastery. An experience of competency can be attained through facilitating adventure-based problem-solving initiatives in such a way as to set the group up for success. Because most ABC experiences require effort, participants' self-efficacy is boosted.

Finally, stage six is Poise, which suggests a state of inner balance as well as a sense of unity among team members. Think of an athlete in top form. We might say that they are poised to perform well. This feeling of inner calm is the culmination of the prior five stages of shared enjoyment. What therapist wouldn't want their clients to leave treatment feeling poised to take on the rest of life's adventures?

CBT AND DBT

ABC can be easily used to support the principles of CBT and DBT, two widely accepted treatment models. For example, many of the problem-solv-

Providing a solid foundation. *Photo by Ben Silverman.*

ing activities presented in this book require group members to reframe their thinking in order to be successful. Shifting one's thinking is the central tenet of CBT (Ellis, 1996), and ABC allows participants to implement the process immediately, in effect giving clients practice for real-life situations. Some ABC activities require shifting one's thinking from a competitive to a cooperative paradigm in order to attain a successful outcome; this shift can likewise be useful in building and maintaining personal and professional relationships.

Similarly, skills practiced through ABC highlight central tenets of DBT, a popular treatment model that has gained good empirical support (Aguire, 2013). DBT emphasizes skills such as emotional regulation and mindfulness. Patients in DBT groups are often asked to pause and take note of their emotions. Van der Kolk (2014) and Roth (2004) agree that knowing what we are thinking and feeling are the keys to getting better through psychotherapy. ABC provides ample opportunities for such self-reflection as the activities often bring about feelings of joy, fear, or frustration. These emotions are ubiquitous in life, and having opportunities to recognize and express them in treatment is highly transferable to other contexts. I often pause after an activity to ask group members how they are feeling, especially when hearty laughter has occurred. Likewise, if participants become upset during a particularly stimulating activity, the principles of mindfulness that are central to DBT can be used to help the individuals regain relative calm.

Treatment Planning Goals (CBT)

1. Client practiced increasing tolerance for frustration and identified specific areas where doing so would be helpful.
2. Client practiced asking for help from supportive peers and identified specific applications to help address targeted behavior.
3. Client engaged in creative problem-solving activities and reflected on other areas where doing so would be useful.
4. Client provided direct assistance to peers when it was requested.
5. Client engaged in creative problem-solving activities and explored other areas that would benefit from collaborative problem-solving.
6. Client practiced asking for and accepting help and discussed other situations when doing so would be useful.

Treatment Planning Goals (DBT)

1. Client practiced affect regulation while engaging in problem-solving tasks.
2. Client practiced positive self-talk.

INSURANCE ISSUES

The Outdoor Behavioral Healthcare Council has recently been successful in getting a service code for Outdoor Behavioral Healthcare/Wilderness Therapy (1006) accepted by several insurance companies, but this is for long-term wilderness therapy, and not for the kinds of activities described in this book. Programs that are certified to bill for partial hospitalization programs (PHP), intensive outpatient programs (IOP), or residential treatment can use ABC as one of the treatment modalities being offered. Those working in private practice settings need to use the service code for group psychotherapy (90853). The challenge with this is that each unit of group therapy is for a one-hour or 90-minute session, and most insurance companies only allow one unit per day. This is fine if you are using activities from part II of this book. If you want to offer a full ABC treatment day, as described in part III, at this point there is no way to bill third-party payers for this service if you are not authorized to bill for IOP or PHP services. One option might be to offer a daylong program like Recovery Adventure Day (RAD) in smaller one-hour segments over a longer period of time.

Since CBT and DBT have more evidence-based support than ABC currently does, adventure-based methods can be framed so that they are consistent with the principles and goals associated with the more widely accepted modalities for billing purposes. By contextualizing the activities this way, as indicated above, the requirements of third-party payers and regulatory boards are likely to be satisfied.

RELATIONSHIP BETWEEN THERAPIST AND PARTICIPANTS

When a traditionally trained therapist introduces adventure activities, they need to be aware that doing so may change the therapeutic relationship between themselves and their group members. Specifically, presenting your group members with opportunities to continually push themselves by trying new things means that at some point they may experience having failed in front of you. This could stimulate feelings of shame in them. Similarly, some participants may have negative associations with some of the activities used in ABC. They could be reminded of gym class or summer camp, and if they have negative associations with those experiences, they may have an adverse reaction to what they might perceive as silly games. I suggest you invite such individuals to fully express their displeasure. Remind them that they can choose to observe at any point if they prefer, but also remind them that you may be offering them a different experience: they also have the option of participating with all of their skepticism. The old maxim "Start where the group is" may be applicable. A gentle approach is likely to serve both you and your group members best.

Ringer and Gáspár (2017) observe that the addition of physical challenges to psychologically oriented contexts has the potential to enrich therapeutic connotations while at the same time introduce the potential for destructive defensiveness to occur. The authors maintain that the integrated model carries the potential for increased acting-out behavior as members may mistake physical tasks as the primary area of focus when in fact they are intended to support the primary task of growth and change during ABC events. Wright (2005) concurs that it is vital for the group worker using activities not to lose sight of the primary therapeutic purpose of the group. Group leaders and members alike can become so involved in an activity that they can lose sight of the group's primary purpose.

Therapists can potentially soften group members' resistance to getting involved in ABC through their own active participation in some of the activities. In that sense, ABC is a more egalitarian model than most forms of psychotherapy in which the therapist behaving similarly to their client would constitute an abdication of the therapeutic role and be counter-therapeutic, if not unethical. Since much of the behavior called for in ABC is physical and nonverbal, a different paradigm applies. I want my group members to know that I am not asking them to do anything that I am not willing to do myself. I convey this behaviorally by participating in many of the more playful activities while still maintaining my therapeutic role. For example, though I will demonstrate that I am willing to take constructive risks, accept help, and at times look silly in front of my group members, I would be less likely to delve into my own intrapsychic challenges in front of the group as doing so would potentially undermine my therapeutic value to the participants. However, seeing the facilitator as fully human can have an inviting effect and may allow group members to express themselves more freely, allowing the facilitator to see what roles they gravitate toward.

Cytrynbaum (2014), citing Horwitz, says that group members unconsciously opt for specific roles. In families, an individual often volunteers to be the "problem child," and in so doing they may allow the rest of the family to behave as if they are problem-free. The family can be said to be "locating" the collective problems in one family member (Roth, 2004). Role flexibility is a desirable quality in a healthy group or family. Adventure-based therapists will often structure programming to bring such role flexibility about. For example, a facilitator might choose to blindfold an overly controlling group or family member during an activity so as to encourage leadership among other members of the group. (Note that I use the terms "group leader," "adventure-based therapist," and "facilitator" interchangeably throughout the text. This use of multiple terms is reflective of the multifaceted roles played and concomitant skills employed by therapists using ABC interventions.)

Crafty interventions such as the one mentioned above might provoke the group members to view you in a more antagonistic way rather than the supportive way in which therapists are often experienced. For example, if you enforce a consequence by taking away a resource or deducting seconds during a timed challenge, you may be experienced as punitive, and this can lead to regressive behavior in the group. I suggest you openly explore with your group members all these shifts in how they experience you in your different roles. Finally, ABC lends itself very well to co-leadership, whereby one person can focus on facilitating the activities while the other focuses on dynamics within the group and participants' therapeutic objectives.

TRAINING AND CERTIFICATION

The terms "soft skills" and "hard skills" are commonly used in AT literature to differentiate between knowing the physical setup and safety issues associated with each activity (hard skills) and knowing how to help participants usefully integrate their experience into their therapeutic goals (soft skills).

For clinicians with formal mental health training, the soft skills may come more easily than the technical aspects of the interventions. The hard skills required to lead most of the activities in this book are minimal. Most group leaders should be able to safely direct the activities described without additional training. However, additional training is highly recommended as it may take significant time and experience to become comfortable using ABC methods. You can pursue further training through professional organizations such as the Association for Experiential Education (AEE; www.aee.org) and Project Adventure (www.pa.org). See the appendix for additional suggestions.

Training in the use of adventure activities is not standardized. The advantage to this is that there are many ways to obtain training and experience. The downside is that it's hard to tell how much training someone has had without actually talking to the person. Training in outdoor team-building equipment is easier to obtain than training for portable activities, though many people who offer training for challenge course programs include portable activities too. The designers of challenge courses (synonymous with ropes courses) offer such training, and in many cases the host organizations will offer their own training. The Association of Challenge Course Technology (www.acctinfo.org) has established two levels of certification for those who want to facilitate programming that includes high and low ropes course challenges. For therapists who would like to focus their learning on using portable activities that can be used indoors, there is no standard certification available at this time, though many training options are available.

Note that the AEE, the Association of Challenge Course Technology, and the Outdoor Behavioral Health Council (https://obhcouncil.org) each hold annual conferences. These conferences offer abundant opportunities to take workshops in experiential methods with trainers from various disciplines, including education, organizational development, and adventure therapy. There is a subgroup of the AEE called the Therapeutic Adventure Professionals Group. This group offers its own training in addition to those offered at the AEE annual conference. Such gatherings offer opportunities to expand one's range of adventure-oriented techniques. Many organizations that attend these meetings offer their own in-depth training opportunities. Project Adventure is the best known of these. You may also contact me to schedule training specifically in the activities described in the text as well. See the appendix for details.

MATERIALS AND SUPPLIES

A primary feature that distinguishes ABC from other therapeutic modalities is the use of equipment. In addition to augmenting a sense of free expression and the unknown in a group, using props can reveal valuable information about group members. Pat Ogden (2018) notes that "props are our friends." Noticing how group members hold or use an object can quickly reveal how anxious, aggressive, or playful they may be feeling. One of the challenges associated with using equipment is acquiring it.

Most of the materials needed for the activities in this book can be purchased and/or constructed with items that can be found at stores such as Target, hardware stores, and online. Companies dedicated to selling team-building equipment are also good resources (see the appendix for details). These are good options for those who do not have the time or energy to acquire their own props for each activity. A kit containing all the materials needed to facilitate most of the activities in this book and all the activities in chapter 18: Recovery Adventure Day is available through www.adventureforwardtherapy.com and https://training-wheels.com, both listed in the appendix.

Part II

ABC in Outpatient Mental Health Settings

Chapter Four

Overview of a Session

Part II consists of twelve activity sequences, each based on a specific theme and material used. Part III describes a longer sequence of activities designed to support people in recovery from addiction. These can be done as one daylong program or broken down into a series of shorter chunks. Each chapter stands on its own and offers a logical sequence of activities, beginning with an icebreaker and progressing to increasingly more difficult problem-solving challenges. Though I recommend that the activities within each chapter be done in order, the chapters can be used in any order, and the activities within each chapter can be combined to meet the needs of a particular group.

Each session begins with a Question of the Day (QOD) that is reflective of that day's theme. The QODs can be answered in round-robin format. This establishes a tone of joining-in and acceptable risk taking. These daily questions are somewhat whimsical and designed to invite group members to think about and share their preferences, thoughts, and other unique aspects of themselves. A number of these questions were inspired by Larry Eckert (1998), who has written a book that contains over 1,000 discussion-provoking questions. The process of risk-taking and joining-in is usually more meaningful than the actual content of the answers. It's okay if people want to pass as you want to establish a sense of autonomy in your group members.

After the QOD, a progression of activities increasing in difficulty is described. I have followed Middleman's (1980) suggestion to plan sequences that move from simple to more complex, and from leader-centered to group-centered. Since the membership at many programs changes frequently, the first activity in each session following the QOD includes a review of people's names. These Name Games are followed by activities that emphasize inclusiveness and fun, with several problem-solving challenges concluding each session. Comer and Hirayama (2009) suggest that activities be sequenced so that those used during the beginning stages of a group help to establish norms of jumping in and building supportive relationships. The QODs and Name Games that begin each session are designed to accomplish these goals. Comer and Hirayama (2009) add that middle-stage activities help to sustain groups by providing opportunities for conflict management and shared problem-solving. The more complex challenges that constitute the bulk of each session provide such opportunities.

I add Processing Points following the description of each activity. It is important that participants use their experience in the group to advance their therapeutic goals. The Processing Points are intended to help integrate group members' lived experience with their therapeutic aims. Comer and Hirayama (2009) caution the worker using activities not to become overly focused on the activities themselves, as in doing so they could lose sight of the primary therapeutic task of the group. The Processing Points help to avoid this potential oversight. In addition to the open-ended questions that I suggest, it is advisable for practitioners to develop a second set of questions based specifically on a particular group's approach to a given activity. Simpson, Miller, and Bocher (2006) suggest that such impromptu processing is likely to be more attuned to group members' specific treatment goals.

Each session functions therapeutically on two levels: group members will be having *fun*, which is immediately therapeutic, and the insights gleaned will pay dividends going forward. The novelty factor alone will engender a sense of discovery in the group, but even more important, it sends a tacit message that there are many ways to look at any given situation or life event. This message is the crux of most cognitive-behavioral interventions (Ellis, 1996). The corrective message is conveyed indirectly as the group becomes involved in each activity, but it is up to the group leader to help members transfer their experience to specific issues in their lives.

I conclude each activity by identifying where I learned it. In some cases, I refer readers to a specific book or author. In other instances, for example, if I learned the challenge at a workshop or training session, I note where I learned that particular activity. Occasionally, I do not cite a source either because an activity is so well established that it can be considered general knowledge or because I have put significant original thinking into the description. But even in these cases, I have learned so much from colleagues in the field that I cannot assume sole credit for any of the activities. I encourage the reader to refer to the original sources for further explanation of the activities and also to experiment with the activities as described and make them your own.

Think of the activities as a means to realizing group members' primary therapeutic outcomes; it is essential to discuss what arose during the activity and how to transfer group members' "here-and-now" experience into other areas of their lives. For example, if multiple attempts are required to complete a given task, where else in life do group members need to be patient with themselves? If role flexibility is called for during an activity, in what other settings might taking on a new role be useful? Did someone trying to change a relative's bad habit refrain from controlling others' behavior during a challenge? If you notice laughter occurring, take time to help group members reflect on what factors enabled them to experience the freedom to laugh. Be on the lookout for ways in which specific group members become liberated from their obsessive thoughts and dysfunctional roles while engaged in the group and draw those cognitive insights to their attention. Remember that the activities are a means to realizing group members' primary therapeutic outcomes. So the pattern of ABC consists of direct experience, reflection, and application to participants' primary treatment issues, a pattern known as the "Adventure Wave" (Schoel, Prouty, & Radcliffe, 1988; Schoel & Maizell, 2002).

I also indicate the approximate time required for each activity. I recommend that you allow flexibility in managing time between activities. Occasionally, one of the activities will lead to a rich therapeutic discussion. When this happens, I suggest that you realize that you have struck gold—no need to move on to the next event as long as you are engaged in productive dialog with your group members.

Think of the activities described in each session as a bag of Lego bricks— not as blocks designed to support one specific sculpture but rather as building blocks to create a unique structure that fits the needs of your group. As you grow increasingly comfortable with the activities and materials, you will have an array of multicolored blocks of various sizes to design a unique adventure-based counseling program. It's as easy as A-B-C!

Chapter Five

"Can" Day

Discovering New Abilities within You

QUESTION OF THE DAY

What "Can" You Do Well? This strengths-based question functions to remind people that though they may be struggling in certain areas of their lives, their life is not a complete loss, and there may be some things that they are quite accomplished at. This question also functions as a segue to the day's programming, all of which uses cans in various ways. This kind of wordplay has the subtle effect of suggesting to group members that there are many ways of looking at something and that sometimes it is easier to change our perspective than it is to change other people, places, and things in our lives. Group members may be surprised at the many things they "can" accomplish.

"CAN" DAY ACTIVITIES

Pass the Can

Materials Needed: Two cans with any sharp edges taped over. Feel free to use anything from an empty soda can to an empty 1-gallon paint can.
Approximate Time: 5–10 minutes
Description: This activity begins as a simple Name Game in case group members are not acquainted with each other. Ask each person to pass an empty can to the person to their immediate right while saying the person's name, as in "Here, Rachel." However, they may only use their arms *from the elbow up*. After the circle is completed, ask your group members to do the same thing, only this time using their feet to pass the can. If the can falls to

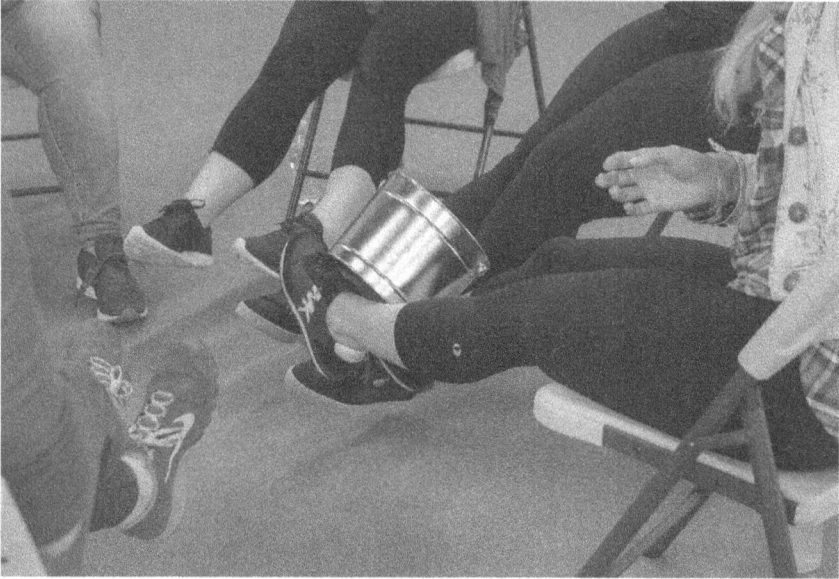

Passing the can. *Photo by Ben Silverman.*

the ground, pick it up and start again until the can makes it around the whole circle. The final round can involve one can being passed with the feet in one direction, while another can gets passed in the opposite direction using arms, with names being repeated along with each pass.

Processing Points: This activity involves multitasking and presents an opportunity to talk about where else in life multitasking presents challenges. It also fosters a sense of novelty and a willingness to try something new. This idea alone could constitute a whole therapy hour. Where else in life would group members like to try doing something differently?

In the Can

Materials Needed: One large (2 lb.) empty coffee can, or an empty 1-gallon paint can, or the equivalent, and one object that is small enough to easily fit inside the can but large enough to hold in a variety of ways. I often use a small stuffed animal or a Beanie Baby.

Approximate Time: 10 minutes

Description: In the Can is an activity whereby group members deposit a small stuffed animal into a large can using any part of their bodies except their forearms and hands. Feel free to allow one of the group members to give the stuffed animal a name. Let's call him "Elmer." Although participants may not use their hands to propel Elmer, they may use their hands to set him in his starting position. This could be under somebody's chin, for example, or under their upper arm. After a couple of examples, ask the group to set a goal by stating how many unique ways they can deposit Elmer into his home. For most groups, a goal of 20–30 novel ways is reasonable.

There are many ways to go about this activity and many useful ways of talking about the process. The variations of a single person attempting the challenge usually become exhausted after 10 or 12 attempts. Some people in the group are likely to generate more ideas than others, while others might be more willing to try implementing the suggestions. There may be opportunities for the "idea generators" to collaborate with the "doers." Using pairs or trios is often a viable option for reaching the group's goal.

Processing Points: You can ask questions such as "Where else in your life have you benefited from collaboration?" or "In what areas of your life might you benefit from working more collaboratively?" Another useful question might be "When do we get attached to doing something one way when there could be many viable options?"

Low frustration tolerance (LFT) can be addressed using this activity when the group begins to run out of ideas. Also, there are opportunities to talk about integrity as the group members evaluate the originality of each transfer.

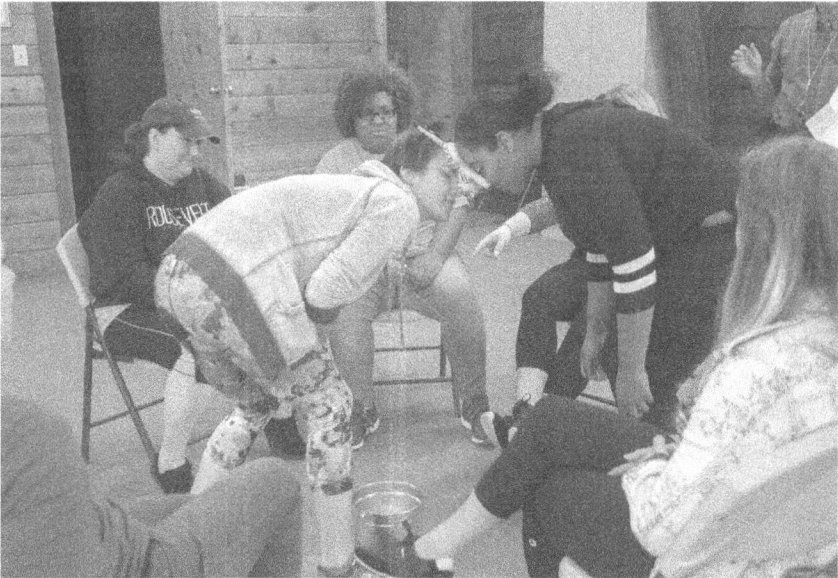

Depositing Elmer into his home. *Photo by Ben Silverman.*

Sometimes issues concerning personal space become relevant during this activity. For example, if Elmer were placed between two group members' cheeks, there might be an opportunity to talk about proxemics and the many issues associated with personal space. If you are working with children, they might need to be prompted to experiment in forming partners or trios. Most schools stress individual work over collaboration, so some prompting by the therapist might be warranted. You can then have a broader discussion about the advantages and possible drawbacks of collaboration in other contexts.

Source: Steve Simpson at a TEAM conference in 1998.

All Touch

Materials Needed: One empty can (a 4-oz. can for groups of 20 or more). Smaller cans or other objects will work for smaller groups. I have used the top of a dry erase marker for groups of eight to 12 with great results. A thimble also works well for smaller groups.

Approximate Time: 5 minutes

Description: This simple activity involves asking everyone in the group to make physical contact with an object *without making contact with each other*. Obviously, the smaller the object, the greater the challenge. Adjust object size according to number of participants. I usually start by setting the object on the ground and then describing the challenge. The group may soon discover that they need to pick the object up in order to proceed. (Refer to the From "That's impossible" to "We did it!" figure in chapter 18).

Processing Points: There are opportunities here to talk about making sacrifices on behalf of the group. Did specific group members make helpful contributions? What factors contributed to the group's success? What roles emerged during the activity?

Source: Rohnke, 1984.

Target Toss

Materials Needed: One empty 2-lb. coffee can or an empty 1-gallon paint can; beanbags or other objects small enough to be tossed into the can; and some blindfolds

Approximate Time: 25 minutes, depending upon the size of your group (about 5 minutes per pair)

Description: First, place the empty can about five to six feet from the group members, who can be seated in a semicircle. Hand out the beanbags and give group members an opportunity to practice tossing them into the can. Next, explain that each group member will have an opportunity to receive help from someone. This someone can be another group member or a staff member who will assist them in tossing the beanbag into the can while blindfolded. It's up to the individual to choose from whom they would like to receive this assistance. Explain that whoever they choose will act as their coach and will help them find the target kinesthetically, offering suggestions for improvement after each attempt.

After the thrower has been blindfolded, the can may be moved slightly to increase the difficulty (or not—just repeating the process without seeing may be enough of a challenge). Then the blindfolded group member has an unlimited number of opportunities to toss the beanbag into the can while the coach gives instruction and guidance. The coach can return the beanbag to the tosser after each miss. Some people will become frustrated as they try to adapt to the limitations of not being able to see the target; they need to rely more on their listening and the tactile experience of tossing the object. Group members are usually engaged by watching one another attempt this task. They often develop increased empathy for one another by having shared the experience.

Processing Points: Talk about what it felt like to attempt the task, how the assistants were selected, and what feelings or self-talk arose following failed attempts. Where else in our lives are we self-critical, and are there other, friendlier ways, we might want to talk to ourselves? Most people in treatment are highly self-critical, so take plenty of time to talk about the benefits of tolerating frustration and practicing affirming self-talk.

Toxic Waste

Materials Needed: One 15-foot length of rope, a rubber bracelet such as those used for social movements such as the Livestrong campaign, several 5-foot pieces of string, a tennis ball with a face drawn on it, and a receptacle such as a tin can that is large enough to hold the tennis ball

Approximate Time: 15 minutes

Description: Make a loose circle on the floor out of the length of rope and place the tennis ball and the tin can on the floor in the middle of the circle. Explain that "Tennie" has found herself in a dangerous situation. She is traveling and has found herself in an area that is full of bars and business acquaintances who love to drink. She needs to get to an AA meeting, which is represented by the tin can. However, it would be far too dangerous for any of the group members to venture into that territory by themselves. They may, however, use the materials on hand to help get Tennie to a meeting. No group member may enter the roped-off area, or make contact with it at all, for their own safety.

Processing Points: This activity provides an opportunity to talk about what potentially slippery situations members of your group are likely to find themselves in. How might they prepare for the tests that inevitably will arise as they transition from treatment into living a productive life, and what resources will they use to help them though these tests?

Toxic Waste setup. *Photo by the author.*

Chapter Six

Noodle Day

Using Your Noodle for Positive Change and Growth

The term "using your noodle" is commonly used to refer to someone using their brain creatively or effectively. In addition to being a metaphor for one's brain, noodles are, of course, a type of food, and they are also the name given to the long foam cylindrical objects used as flotation devices. It's this last type of noodle that is the material used for the sequence of activities described in this chapter. Chris Cavert and Sam Sikes (1997; 2002) have written two books filled with activities using pool noodles. The novelty factor of these objects alone brings joy to those who play with them.

QUESTION OF THE DAY

What is an idea you have learned in treatment that you have found to be helpful? Please share a situation in which you were able to draw on the idea. CBT and DBT are two popular forms of cognitively oriented treatment, and 12 Step programs, while spiritually oriented, are filled with cognitive constructs such as "One day at a time," "One drink is too many and 100 isn't enough," and so on. Ask your group members to share a concept from treatment or recovery and ask them to give an example of how the idea has been helpful to them. Repetition is an important component of all cognitive therapies, so this exercise in review is likely to be helpful to all concerned. Your group members can borrow freely from each other's good ideas.

NOODLE DAY ACTIVITIES

This sequence of activities uses foam pool noodles, which can be purchased online or at most dollar stores during the warmer months. They are considered seasonal items, but they have year-round use in ABC! The variety of things one can do with a pool noodle outside of water far exceeds those things that can be done while swimming. I use what Cavert and Sikes (1997, 2002) call "midaroni" noodles, or one large pool noodle cut in half to make two shorter noodles, each about three feet long. Because there are so many useful noodle activities, I have included more than can be done in a one-hour group session, so you will need to select according to which ones best meet the needs of your group.

Pass It To

Materials Needed: One noodle
Approximate Time: 5 minutes
Description: This is a quick Name Game that is great for groups of people who are getting acquainted with one another, but because of the fast pace, it is also effective with more established groups. Ask your group members to sit in a circle, either on the floor with their knees up or seated in chairs. One person starts by standing in the center. This is generally the group leader to begin. Explain that the person in the center will attempt to (gently) swat the shins of various group members with a noodle, one at a time, according to when their name is called. One person sitting in the circle is elected to begin calling names. They should say, "Pass it to _____," naming one of the group members. The person in the center must then try to swat the named person's calf before the named person can say, "Pass it to _____," naming yet another group member, and so on. Whenever the person in the center makes contact with a group member before they can say "Pass it to _____," that person becomes the new person in the center and hence becomes the next swatter. If any one group member is in the center for too long, you can try tightening the circle a bit. Also, if a group member flinches to avoid being tagged, that person goes to the center!
Processing Points: This one offers a good opportunity for group members to reflect on their feelings. The fast action can engender feelings of nervousness and excitement. The point is to allow for reflection and increased awareness of any feelings that arise.
Source: Cavert and Sikes, 1997.

Circle Drop

Materials Needed: One noodle for each group member

Approximate Time: 10–15 minutes

Description: Group members stand in a circle, all facing the same direction (for example, to the right) with about two feet between them. Each person should be holding a noodle upright inside the circle, using the forefinger of their left hand. The objective is for the group to simultaneously take a step forward while letting go of one noodle and catching the one in front of them that the person they are following has just let go of. The challenge is for each person to catch the noodle of the person in front of them before that noodle falls to the ground. Can the group make it all the way around without any drops? That is the goal.

Processing Points: There are many things that you might want to discuss in conjunction with this activity. For example, catching and letting go of noodles during each step can be a metaphor for talking and listening, giving and receiving, etc. Also, frustration can be a factor here. How are group members managing their frustration? Where else in life is this an issue? Are some noodles easier to balance than others? Given that not all the noodles will have been cut exactly straight across (this is often the case), there may be a temptation to blame the victim when a particular noodle gets dropped. Where else in life do victims get blamed?

Source: Cavert and Sikes, 1997.

Pick Up Sticks

Materials Needed: 12–15 noodles of various colors

Approximate Time: 10 minutes

Description: This is a variation of the classic game Pick Up Sticks, but rather than using narrow wooden sticks, we're going to use pool noodles. The group leader drops the "sticks" in the center of the circle, and group members work alone or in pairs (think about what makes the most sense from a clinical point of view) to try to remove the "sticks" without moving any others. Each time a stick is successfully taken away, the player(s) get another turn.

Processing Points: You can talk about integrity during this activity as group members may have been inclined to overlook small movements of the noodles. Discuss situations in which it is important to be exacting and others in which it is advisable to overlook minor errors. Also, what memories were brought on by the game? Did people play Pick Up Sticks when they were young? How are their fine motor skills, and what is different about playing the game with a different material?

Working in sync. *Photo by the author.*

Pass the Pasta

Materials Needed: Four noodles (two of one color and two of another color)

Approximate Time: 10 minutes

Description: This rousing game invariably gets the group laughing and engaged. Group members should be seated in a circle. Explain to the group that the task is to pass a noodle to the person seated two people to their right. The person passing the noodle should say "Watch it, _____!" while saying the name of the person receiving the noodle. The person who receives the noodle passes it to the person seated two people to their right and so on until the noodle makes it all the way around the circle. The fun really begins when additional noodles are introduced. I usually introduce a second noodle after the first one has gone around a couple of times so that two noodles are in motion at once. Then I pause and use a different color noodle to be passed in the opposite direction. Then I add another in that direction. Can you tell where this is going? Yes, you are right, the final challenge is for the group to pass *two* noodles in each direction simultaneously!

This game tends to get chaotic. You can modulate the level of chaos by deciding how many new noodles to introduce. Having an odd number of people in the group insures that every group member will receive noodles from each direction. You can use yourself (in or out) to create an odd number of players (see photo in chapter 3).

Processing Points: This activity is mostly designed to engender an experience of fun. I had one adolescent group member remark after a lively game of Pass the Pasta that she was having an otherworldly experience, as if she were "here yet not here." Having the experience of laughing and having fun is in itself therapeutic. Encourage your group members to reflect on other times they found themselves temporarily freed of their worries. Or if the chaos was upsetting to people, you can explore the self-care techniques they used to manage the anxiety.

Source: Cavert and Sikes, 1997.

Stick Puzzles

Materials Needed: 11 or more midaronies

Approximate Time: 10 minutes

Description: Stick Puzzles can be done on a tabletop by one person alone using matchsticks or pencils for the sticks. Using pool noodles enlarges the playing area and makes the puzzles more inviting for several people to engage in at once. One such activity is called Nine Lines. Place six noodles side by side vertically on the ground, each about 18 inches apart. Give the group five additional noodles to work with and ask if they can make the number nine by adding the five noodles to the six, without moving the original six noodles. There are two possible solutions to this puzzle. One involves using two noodles to make a plus sign and adding the three noodles after it. The other solution involves placing the five noodles to form two *N*s (by placing a noodle diagonally between two sets of two lines) and an *E* (by attaching three noodles horizontally to the last line).

Another puzzle that involves looking at something from a different point of view is called Five Triangles. Make a large triangle using nine noodles. Ask your group members to move only five of the nine noodles to create five triangles from the one large one.

These puzzles will be more easily solved by those who are able to think creatively and who may have had experience attempting similar kinds of puzzles.

Processing Points: Any puzzle or activity that entails looking at things from an alternative point of view has immediate application to therapeutic traditions like CBT. See chapter 2 for more on this. Give your group members an opportunity to talk directly about a situation that they have successfully used CBT to address, or a situation in which they are stuck and could benefit from some alternative perspectives. Work with these situations, perhaps taking some time between the two puzzles for some straightforward CBT with a couple of group members. Does the way they approach their difficulties in life mirror the way they approach these puzzles? What part of their process could be improved upon?

Source: Project Adventure Table Top Backpack.

Noodle Drawings

Materials Needed: Plenty of noodles
Approximate Time: 15 minutes
Description: In this exercise you will offer your group members a chance to "draw" using noodles instead of markers or pens. Can they use the available noodles to "draw" a house on the floor? What about a boat or a horse? What other figures can the group construct using just the noodles?

Processing Points: Did group members limit themselves because they don't think of themselves as artists? Who stepped forward to create the images and who stayed in the background? Give your group members an opportunity to reflect on the choices they made. Did the group use all of its resources in creating the images? How did these decisions get made? Where else in life is using more material not always the best choice? Think about cooking with oil, for example, or spending time in the sun.

Human Knot

Materials Needed: One noodle for each group member
Approximate Time: 5–15 minutes
Description: This is variation on the classic team-building challenge of the same name, but instead of group members joining hands to begin, each

person is connected to two other group members by a noodle. Ask the group members to stand in a circle. Give one noodle to each person and ask them to hold the noodle in their right hand and extend it into the middle of the circle. Each person should use their left hand to grab the end of another person's noodle according to the following criteria:

1. You cannot connect to the person to your immediate right or left.
2. You must be connected to two different people; that is, you must grab the noodle of someone other than the person who has taken the end of your noodle.

The challenge is for the group to become untangled without anyone letting go of a noodle. This requires a lot of teamwork and creative problem-solving. Using noodles allows the group to engage in a high-level challenge without people feeling as though their personal space is being violated. Some programs have a "no touching" policy, and the use of noodles in Human Knot allows this policy to be maintained.

There are several possible outcomes to this activity. Groups are usually successful in becoming untangled, with all group members facing inward or out, but untangled either way. Sometimes the untangled group will be in two separate circles. This is an acceptable outcome and might invite a conversation about other instances in which a group needs to divide into two smaller groups in order to be successful. For example, companies often need to work in subgroups, and families sometimes need to break up. There are times when the knot will prove too difficult to untangle. In this case the group may need to make one minor rule-bending adjustment in order to untangle itself. In rare cases a group finds itself completely stuck. In such cases, you can discuss other instances in which acceptance and surrender are viable answers to a sticky situation. Powerlessness over an addictive behavior may be one such example, and contending with a stubborn person may be another (see chapter 18).

Processing Points: What other "knots" have group members experienced in their lives and how could some of the same problem-solving techniques that the group used during this activity be transferred to other settings? What would it look like to have the support of the entire group? Did group members become frustrated during the activity? Where else have they experienced frustration and how did they cope with it? What else came up for people during the activity, and what does the experience remind them of?

Whether or not the knot gets untangled may be less important than how the group goes about the task. Do people seem to be working at cross-purposes or is there a sense of shared focus? Leaders will often emerge during this challenge as some people have better spatial perception than others and may more easily see a way out of the collective mess. How are the leaders' suggestions taken up by the group? You can draw analogies between how the group works through the knot and how they help each other untangle the psychological knots they have created in their lives.

Cube Pass

Materials Needed: 12 midaronies
Approximate Time: 15 minutes
Description: This two-part challenge involves the group first forming a cube out of the 12 noodles. How many people does it take to form a cube that can be suspended in the air while maintaining its shape? The second part of the challenge is to have as many group members as possible pass through the cube without touching it. Passing through the cube means entering through one of the sides and coming out any other side. A pass-through does not necessarily need to be directly opposite the side that was entered. Can all of the group members pass through the cube? This would require role flexibility, as a person cannot both pass through the cube and support it at the same time.

Processing Points: How did the group members decide who would initially build and hold the cube and who would pass through it? How did the number of people involved in making and holding the cube get negotiated? Did it seem as though the task had an appropriate number of people involved, or were there too few or too many? What other situations have group members experienced that were either over- or understaffed?

This activity is also useful for talking about integrity. Did the group leave it up to the facilitator to judge whether or not those passing through the cube had touched the noodles? You can use this topic as a way to broach the subject of self-initiative for treatment and self-evaluation of one's progress.

Noodle Jousting

Materials Needed: Two noodles, two or more blindfolds, and two pieces of rope or alternate boundary markers
Approximate Time: 10–20 minutes
Description: Divide the group into two subgroups of equal number. Each group should be standing behind a piece of rope or alternate boundary marker. There should ideally be 20–30 feet or more between the two groups (this activity works best in an outdoor setting or in a large indoor space). Explain that the task is for one player from each team to be blindfolded and given a noodle. The two "jousters" head toward the playing area simultaneously. Each player tries to be the first to strike his opponent with the pool noodle. Whoever does "wins" that round. Strikes should be shoulder level or below and not aimed at the head. Since both players are blindfolded, they need to

take their cues from their fellow team members. Give everyone in the group an opportunity to be in the center, and respect people's choice to remain in a supporting role. Very often those who are reluctant at first will grow more willing as they see others attempt the task.

Processing Points: Was it hard to tune in to the voices of one's coaches given that there were people talking on both sides? How did group members meet this challenge? Where else have they had to listen carefully? What was it like to feel dependent on their fellow group members for directions? Again, where else do they turn for support in their lives? Finally, though the actual risk during this activity is low, the perceived risk can feel significant (losing in front of one's peers, getting struck, etc.). Where else in life would group members like to take a calculated risk?

Old One Tooth

Materials Needed: One or more noodles

Approximate Time: 10–15 minutes

Description: The best way to describe this activity is to think of a dragon chasing its own tail. Each group of six to 10 people forms a single-file line. For groups that can tolerate physical contact, each person holds the shoulders of the person in front of him. In situations in which touch is to be minimized or avoided altogether, noodles can be used to connect group members. The person at the front attempts to swat the behind of the last person in the line, and he tries to avoid being struck. Obviously, the people in the middle of the line are put in a difficult position. The closer to the middle, the more divided a person's loyalties might become. Once the person on the end has been hit, the person in front becomes the tail and the next person takes a turn being the "tooth" at the front. Allow everyone in the group to have a turn at the front and back positions. Allow about one minute per chase before changing positions.

Processing Points: Although the attention during this activity tends to be on the people at either end of the line, I have found that the richest discussions usually emerge from the experience people have had being in the center. Though the activity tends to be fun initially, it can lead to some painful memories of feeling caught between two opposing parties. Being the child of divorcing parents comes to mind as one such example, but there are many others: answering to two bosses at work, taking guidance from people with different opinions, and so on. You can discuss how people manage these dual alliances and where else in life that struggle appears.

Source: Cavert and Sikes, 1997.

Chasing our own tail. *Photo by Ben Silverman.*

Bonus Activity: Ventilation of Emotion

Put a pool noodle in someone's hands and one of their first instincts will be to swat at something. Why not put this instinct to good use and make some room for your group members to ventilate some of their pent-up frustration and anger? The noodle can be held in one hand or two and then simply swatted repeatedly on the ground. Ventilation of emotion is often associated with Gestalt therapy, and catharsis is cited as one of the 11 therapeutic factors of group psychotherapy (Yalom & Leszcz, 2005). The Gestalt tradition of emotional ventilation focuses on an individual's ability to express rather than repress difficult emotions such as rage and aggression. The idea of cathartic moments emanating from interpersonal group psychotherapy refers primarily to culminations of challenging interactions with a group that may lead one to get in touch with and express challenging feelings, much like in Gestalt therapy, the main difference being the group setting as opposed to an individual therapeutic context.

The emotional ventilation exercise here capitalizes on the cacophony of the group ventilating in unison. Much of the self-consciousness associated with expressing anger may disappear when one's own voice is just one among a chorus of voices. Large group self-awareness training such as Lifespring, Erhard Training Seminars, and the Hoffman Institute make use of this shame-ameliorating effect of group life. I ask my group members to think of some behavior or relationship that they are ready to let go of. I ask them to think of an idea or a person that is no longer contributing to their well-being. This could be "negative thinking," an abusive partner, or self-downing ideas. I ask the group members to literally crush the object of their discontent during this exercise.

Emotional ventilation can be used as an interlude between problem-solving activities. Look for opportune moments to introduce it, for example in a group when half or more of your group members seem to be experiencing unhelpful thoughts or are remaining in destructive relationships.

I had planned a progression of noodle games such as those described above. There were six group members present, most of whom were contending with potentially self-sabotaging thoughts or circumstances. For example, one group member who had been sober from alcohol for several months said that her boyfriend of two years was persisting in bringing beer into their apartment even after she had repeatedly requested that he refrain from doing so. Another group member had recently broken up with a boyfriend who was similarly unsympathetic. One of the men in the group reported that his roommate was engaged in self-destructive behavior on a daily basis and the patient maintained that he was trying to let go of changing his roommate's behavior. Another group member talked about a planned relapse, and another complained about how challenging it was for him to try to hang out at the bar with old friends while remaining sober himself. Collectively, the group was experiencing a great deal of the frustration that is often associated with the trials of early recovery. This seemed like an ideal moment to give the group an opportunity to ventilate their collective frustration that they had been describing. The ventilation of emotion seemed to help because I presented the Human Knot challenge just afterward, and the group's focus and concentration were outstanding as the group members had symbolically disentangled themselves from pesky human entanglements. I suspect that had the group attempted the Human Knot activity without having had a chance to directly express some of their pent-up emotion, they would have become much more easily frustrated by the problem-solving challenge.

Chapter Seven

Ball Day

So Long, Gym Class; Hello, Self-Acceptance

Perhaps more so than any other object, balls conjure images of gym class and competitive sporting activities. For some people these are happy memories, but for others gym class and associated mandated sporting events trigger feelings of humiliation and self-doubt. The activities described below are primarily cooperative in nature. Some emphasize the fun factor while others are more challenging. Together, they offer group members a new set of associations with the simple, round objects commonly known as balls. These new associations may be in and of themselves therapeutic because they allow people to experience in vivo that change is possible.

You will need a variety of balls for the activities described here, including very soft cloth balls and beach balls. Enjoy the play!

QUESTION OF THE DAY

What memories do you have of gym class? Gym class is often regarded by administrators and students as a silly requirement. Most often, no time for reflection is allowed. Therefore, students are denied an opportunity to talk about their experience, regardless of whether it was enjoyable or painful. Some group members may have experienced humiliation at the hands of their gym teachers or classmates. For others, gym class may have been the highlight of their school day. This question gives people an opportunity to express what may be long-suppressed feelings.

BALL DAY ACTIVITIES

7-Up

Materials Needed: One tossable object for each group member (these can be plastic, cloth, or even beanbags). Whatever you use should be relatively easy to catch. I recommend using a variety of objects of various shapes and sizes and one for each group member up to a maximum of seven. Whatever you use should be relatively easy to catch.

Approximate Time: 10 minutes

Description: With your group members standing in a circle, give one person a tossable object and ask them to toss it to another group member while saying that person's name. The receiver then catches the object before returning it to the person who threw it to them. It might be helpful to distinguish a "toss" from a return. In returning the object to the thrower, it can simply be handed to that person, as opposed to thrown again. The facilitator gives a second tossable object to another group member. On the facilitator's count "One, two, three!" both the first and second throwers toss their objects simultaneously while saying the respective names of the people they are throwing them to. Keep introducing additional objects in the same manner, with one object being added each round. Wait until everyone catches their objects before adding another one. Sometimes this will take several attempts. Remember, all the objects need to be thrown at the same time. The task grows increasingly difficult as more objects are added. At a certain point, depending upon the number of people in your group, individuals will need to toss *and* catch an object in a given round.

As the name "7-Up" implies, this activity works well with up to seven players. Seven seems to be about the most objects a group can handle at once, no matter how many players are involved. The more objects in the air at a time, the harder it becomes to avoid collisions.

Processing Points: What makes this activity challenging? Were people more focused on catching or on throwing? Watch out for blaming when an object falls to the ground. Any game that involves catching and throwing works as a metaphor for communication. We tend to blame the receiver of a message when it gets "dropped," but often the way the message was delivered made "catching" it difficult. Offer group members an opportunity to talk about instances in which they have been part of a dropped message or a misunderstanding. Were they unfairly blamed? Also, there are many "messages" in the air at the same time in this activity. This is a good metaphor for modern life, in which we are inundated with text and email messages and the like. How do group members manage all the data in their lives?

You can allow spontaneous metaphors to emerge during this activity. It tends to stimulate references to any chaotic situation that involves feeling engulfed and overwhelmed by too much information. You can then transfer the problem-solving that occurred during the activity to the real-life situations your group members are contending with.

Source: Karl Rohnke at a TEAM conference.

Group Juggling with Water Pass

Materials Needed: One cup filled with water and one tossable object
Approximate Time: 10 minutes
Description: This works well as an alternative to 7-Up when you are working with groups of eight to 12 people. Ask your group members to stand in a circle. They should begin by tossing an object (an easy-to-catch ball or another easily catchable item) and saying the name of the intended receiver of each pass. This should be done in random order so that everyone in the group receives the ball once without anyone getting it twice. Allow the group to practice this for a minute or two until an order is established that meets the criteria stated above. Now pause and ask your group members to pass a cup of water around the circle so that each person hands the cup to the person standing next to them. Next, explain that you would like the group to experiment with doing both of these tasks at once. See how it goes, pause to reflect and discuss ways of adapting, and repeat.

Processing Points: What was it like to have to attend to two things at once (tossing the ball and passing the cup of water)? How did the group adapt to this challenge? Which task got prioritized? Research has shown that we are really only capable of focusing on one thing at a time, so that if we are reading while listening to music, for example, we are primarily focused on one or the other; the same thing goes for driving and talking on the phone. What other examples occur to you, and what impact does multitasking have on each task?

Source: John Conway at a Therapeutic Adventure Professionals Group Best Practices conference in 2013.

Texts and Emails (aka Phones and Faxes)

Materials Needed: One very soft throwable object for each group member. I recommend using the "water bomb" balls that are sold at most dollar stores.
Approximate Time: 10–15 minutes
Description: This is another activity that involves the group managing many pieces of information at once. This activity works best with a group of 12 or more people but can be done with as few as six. Ask the group members to stand in a circle and give each person a soft cloth ball. The group leader explains that the challenge is for one person to stand in the middle of

the circle and try to catch as many balls as they can while all the balls are launched simultaneously. You can demonstrate this by standing in the middle of the circle yourself and asking the group to launch the balls on your count of "One, two, three!" The balls should be tossed underhanded so that they fly with an arc, making it as easy as possible for the person in the center to catch them.

Give each person in the group an opportunity to be the person in the middle. After a few attempts, it will become apparent that the task of catching all the balls at once is unmanageable. Allow the group members to explore new and novel ways of going about the task. This might involve working in pairs or small groups of three or four, using clothing, and so on. The two rules that need to remain in place are that all the balls need to be launched at the same time and that the group members should remain standing in a circle.

Processing Points: This activity is rich with metaphorical application to mental health recovery. Many questions and analogies emerge naturally as the game is played. For example, where else in life have group members experienced unmanageability? How do group members manage the information overload involved with living in the 21st century? In what ways did the group adapt to the challenge? Can any of these approaches be transferred to other settings (i.e., where and when is it useful to ask for help and use

Coping with an unmanageable situation. *Photo by Ben Silverman.*

creative problem-solving)? Many times people will relate this activity to work environments in which they feel overwhelmed with tasks until they ask for some support from colleagues.

If a group member decides to use a cap or a piece of clothing that can be formed into a receptacle for the balls, you can suggest that by "using a resource," they were successful. What resources can be used to address the primary presenting problem that brought them into treatment? For some people this might be showing up at a program even when they don't feel like it; for others it might be meditation, positive affirmations, or journaling. You can ask what gets in the way of people utilizing the resources they have at their disposal.

Source: Rohnke, 1984.

Moon Ball

Materials Needed: A timer or stopwatch and a beach ball
Approximate Time: 10 minutes
Description: This classic New Game is a great way to get your group warmed up and working collaboratively. The easiest way to envision this activity is to think of it as cooperative volleyball with just one team and no net. The objective is for the group to keep the ball aloft for a specified period of time (one minute, for example) according to the following stipulations:

1. The ball must be tapped or hit from underneath with an open hand.
2. No one may touch the ball two times in a row.
3. Everyone in the group must strike the ball at least once.
4. If the ball hits the ground, the group starts over.

Ideally, this game will be played outdoors or in a room with a high ceiling. While low ceilings present challenges, wind can provide another. Help the group adapt to whatever factors arise and be flexible with the time goal if the original one seems out of reach.

Processing Points: Observe how the group works together and comment on the process that you observe. Did some group members emerge as leaders during the activity? Tolerance for frustration often emerges as a topic for reflection after a group has attempted this challenge multiple times. Talk about where else your group members would like to increase their frustration tolerance.

If and when additional challenges occur, such as gusts of wind, slippery ground cover, or a low ceiling, seize the opportunity to talk about adjusting to conditions or rethinking the approach being taken.

I was leading this activity with a group of young adults in a large group room. The group encountered difficulty with the ball ricocheting off the ceiling. After repeated efforts and mounting frustration, the group eventually decided to attempt the activity while seated. They found success by doing so, and this led to a rich discussion about the need for finding new approaches to work, education, relationships, etc. One group member said that she had attended three conventional four-year colleges before realizing that she was better suited to an alternative learning environment where she was experiencing greater success. Another group member talked about the frustration she felt while remaining in a confrontational relationship with one of her parents. By "sitting down" in the relationship, and not fighting as much, she discovered greater harmony in the relationship with her parent.

Amoeba Tag

Materials Needed: One soft ball that cannot cause injury even if thrown at someone (squishy balls work well for this activity as do balls made out of cloth) and pylons or the equivalent if playing outdoors

Approximate Time: 5 minutes

Description: This game is a variation of the game called Everyone's It. One person starts as "It" and gradually creates a growing cluster of "Its." The way this happens is by the person who is It throwing the ball at other players, who try to avoid being hit. If It misses, the facilitator picks up the ball and returns it to him or her. Once someone is hit with the ball, they are frozen from the waist down and they then become part of the Amoeba (the ever-increasing blob of Its). The Its can then start to work as a team, throwing the ball between them until one of them has a good opportunity to hit another group member, who then is frozen and instantly becomes part of the Amoeba. Gradually all the group members become part of the Amoeba.

Processing Points: This game conjures feelings of inevitability, and allows for a discussion about what other things in life feel inevitable. When working with recovering addicts, I like to use this activity to capture Step 1 of AA's 12 Steps. You might also offer your group members an opportunity to reflect on how they influenced each other during the activity. How did each individual's relationship to other group members change once they became part of the Amoeba? This relates to "in" and "out" group dynamics. Our idea of what any group is like changes once we are on the inside. Can your group members share any such experiences?

Categories

Materials Needed: One rubber "playground" ball or another object that's easy to catch

Approximate Time: 10–15 minutes

Description: Ask your group members to stand in a circle and pass the rubber ball to one another in a random order. Next, explain that you are going to introduce specific categories, and you would like your group members to say an item within each category whenever they receive the ball. The objective is not to repeat an item that has already been said. Practice with a category such as "Colors" or "States within the United States" and then move on to the more expansive categories listed below.

Once the group has grown comfortable with the process, explain that if a group member pauses too long (this is subjective and can be determined by consensus) or repeats an item that has already been stated, he or she will back out of the circle until the following round. I suggest playing each round until about half of your group members remain in the circle. That way those who have gone out do not feel ostracized, nor do they have to wait too long to reenter the group. Some categories to consider:

- Book Titles
- TV Shows
- Movies
- Musical Groups or Performing Artists
- Countries

Processing Points: You may be surprised at the collective knowledge among your group members regarding TV shows, movies, and musical groups. Depending on the age of your participants, you might find that the rounds in these categories go on for much longer than the rounds for books or countries. This offers an opportunity to explore the values and behaviors associated with popular culture. Depending upon your time frame, you might want to take a moment to ask your participants about specific movies, books, or TV shows that have made a meaningful impression on them. As mentioned above, you will learn a lot about the cultural landscape of the groups you are working with though this activity. Adults and older adults may have depth in terms of book titles, whereas young adults and adolescents are likely to have a deeper knowledge of television shows and pop music artists. You can have a meta-analytical discussion with your group about this collective awareness in their cohort.

Fireball

Materials Needed: One medium-size ball. A large rubber "playground" ball, available in general stores and dollar stores, works well.

Approximate Time: 10 minutes

Description: Fireball begins as a simple ball-tossing activity. It evolves into an opportunity for group members to reflect on their judgment of themselves and each other, and it provides an opportunity for group members to increase their sense of integrity.

Ask a group of eight to 15 people to stand in a circle and begin tossing the ball back and forth between them with their non-dominant hand. After group members have become comfortable throwing the ball, announce that you will now introduce some new criteria. Ask the group members to step out of the circle if they feel that they have made a bad toss or a poor catch. The idea here is to emphasize integrity as opposed to self-criticism. In the next round, add the criterion that if anyone makes any extraneous noise or movements they are to step away from the circle. Each time a criterion is added, the reasons to step out of the circle increase. You can introduce the first two criteria one at a time or both at once. Stop each round when there are a few people left and invite those who have stepped out to join in for the following round. If it is taking too long for people to make an error, make the circle a little bigger or speed up the play. For the third round, keep the same criteria, but add, "This time, step out of the circle if you make a bad throw or catch, if you make any extraneous noise or movements, *or* if you judge someone else for having made a poor catch or throw." This invites group members to reflect on ways in which they judge others as well as themselves. Again, stop the round when there are still a few people left.

Play a final round with the added criterion that people will step out of the circle if the group leader points at them. The group leader points at people randomly as the round is being played. This allows the group to compare external and internal messages. Most of us are more comfortable self-monitoring than having an outside authority figure rate our performance.

Processing Points: This activity is highly transferable to other settings and it can lead to some very rich processing. Generally, we are our own worst critics. Often people will step away from the circle and others will have no idea why they did so. On one occasion, a group member actually applauded another member's catch that was juggled momentarily before being caught. The catcher in this instance took himself out of the game at the same moment that the other person was applauding his efforts. Where else in life does this occur? When have people criticized themselves or even given up when others thought they were doing a perfectly good job? This seems to be a fairly common occurrence.

If you are using this game with older adults or others who may have difficulty throwing with their non-dominant hand, feel free to forego the request for them to do so. I have found that the game goes on too long with no errors for most groups when they play with their dominant hand.

Source: Straus, 2016.

Chapter Eight

Word Day

Saying and Playing What You Mean

"Words, words, what are words worth?" the Tom-Tom Club asked in the 1980s. Laurie Anderson sang "Language Is a Virus" during the same decade. Words are the essential means through which 90% of all psychotherapeutic interventions are conducted. We might go so far as to say that words are the very lifeblood of most psychotherapists.

What happens when words are used not as the direct method of therapeutic delivery but rather as toys to be played with? The series of activities presented here uses words in novel ways and allows group members to discover a newfound freedom with language. While each activity offers a means through which group members can build cohesion, work collaboratively, and experiment with new roles, the meta-communication throughout the sequence is that things are not always what they seem to be. This subtle, underlying message may be as helpful as the specific takeaways from each activity. If words are not etched in stone, neither is one's diagnosis.

QUESTION OF THE DAY

Do you have a favorite word, phrase, aphorism, adage, or expression? What is it, and what do you like about it? AA and other 12-step fellowships are rife with pithy aphorisms that are designed to help people stay sober. "One day at a time" was a preexisting idea that was adopted by AA because of its power. Aristotle (1961) wrote that a well-told story should take place within a twenty-four-hour period. Many people find that one day is a period of time that is easy to conceptualize and build goals around. Most of us find that a one-day plan is easier to stick to than a long-range roadmap. Many other expressions are commonly used to support behavioral change. These include "Fake it 'til you make it," "HALT" (when someone is feeling hungry, angry, lonely, or tired), and "The first drink is the one to avoid."

Feel free to offer your group members a list of possible aphorisms that they might want to choose from. These can be geared to developing an outlook that is consistent with their overall goals. Some of my personal favorites are:

Learn from the past. Look to the future. Live in the present.

Comedy is tragedy plus time.

Don't do whatever you like—like whatever you do.

Anxiety is interest paid on trouble before it is due.

An ounce of prevention is worth a pound of cure.

When you smile, the world smiles with you.

WORD DAY ACTIVITIES

Zoom (Race)

Materials Needed: None

Approximate Time: 5 minutes

Description: With group members standing in a circle, say that you are going to pass the word "zoom" around by saying it to the person to your right. That person then says the word to the person to their right and so on until the word gets back around to you. Practice another time, asking the group to pass the word a little faster and louder than they did the first time. Then ask what "zoom" spelled backwards would be. One or more of your group members will say "mooz." You are now going to pass the word "mooz" to your left. Practice a second time. Next, explain that "zoom" and "mooz" are going to have a race. You are going to start both words simultaneously and see which one comes back to you first. You can play several rounds of the race. Usually the person standing opposite the person who starts the race will get hit with both words at approximately the same time, causing confusion. One word will sometimes break down before it makes it around the circle. If this happens, restart the race so that both words make it all the way around. You should have several races, and it's fine to allow group members to begin subsequent races so more people get to experience having both words cross them at nearly the same moment.

Processing Points: When have you gotten hit with two messages at once? What is this experience like and how did you manage it? It can be useful to ask group members which team they identified with more, the "zoom" team or the "mooz" team. It's amazing how quickly people tend to affiliate with a particular side. Subgrouping seems to be part of human nature, and you can use this as a bridge to talk about where else false dichotomies exist when people tend to focus on differences rather than a shared goal of the whole group. Politics and religion are easy targets for this discussion, but what about the world of mental health, in which substance abuse treatment has been segregated from general mental health care? Finally, was there risk involved in this activity? What was it? Was the risk real or perceived? Where else in life does perceived risk get in our way?

Zoom (Improvisation)

Materials Needed: None
Approximate Time: 5 minutes
Description: A second activity that can be done using the same two words as above shifts the focus from the race to spontaneous decision-making. Explain to your group members that they will continue passing the two words around the circle, but this time when the word gets to someone, he or she can either keep passing it along, as in the race game, or make a breaking sound ("Eeeeeeek") and then pass the other word in the opposite direction. If the words get lodged in one section of the circle, you can ask someone in the other part of the circle to begin afresh.

Groups of more than 20 can sometimes handle having two words "in the air" at once, but this increases the challenge significantly and usually results in confusion that leads to at least one of the words deteriorating quickly. It's hard to focus with so much going on around us!

Processing Points: Are you someone who generally goes with the flow, or do you stop to question the status quo? Did this hold true during the activity? What did you notice about roles that people took on in the group? Did a directional conflict occur during the activity? Did two particular people get lodged in a directional conflict? Why do some people seem to butt heads? When is it best to go along and not rock the boat? When is "putting on the brakes" a wise thing to do?
Source: Straus, 2008.

Three-Syllable Game

Materials Needed: None
Approximate Time: 10 minutes
Description: This game is ideal for groups of 12–16 but can work well with as few as eight. Form four small groups of two to four people each (groups of three work best). Explain that each group will take a turn leaving the room for a brief period of time while the other three teams think of a three-syllable word, such as "syl-la-ble." The three groups practice saying the word aloud, with each small group standing in separate corners of the

room and *saying just one syllable each, simultaneously*. So in our "syllable" example, one small group would say "syl," another would say "la," and the third would say "ble," *all at the same time*. The group leader can cue the sounding of the syllables by counting "One, two, three!" The group standing outside the room is then allowed back in and, after hearing the three syllables said in unison, tries to guess the word. If the guessing team needs to hear the word again, they can ask to have it repeated. Each team takes a turn at guessing, and if the timing seems right, a second round can be played, with the words increasing in difficulty. A method that works well for solving the words is to have each member of the guessing team listen carefully to just one of the syllables and then discuss with the other members of their small group. Allow this technique to occur naturally, rather than suggesting it.

Processing Points: How did each small group work together to solve the puzzle? Was there a cooperative spirit and willingness to share resources (clues)? Where else does the same paradigm hold true where each person holds a clue but in order to solve the puzzle, everyone's contribution is valued? Do group members feel that their contributions are valued in their families or work groups? How were the dynamics experienced during this activity similar or different from those they are accustomed to?

Also, it can be useful to reflect on the relationships that emerge between the small groups during this activity. Were hints, clues, and repeats offered freely, or did the groups enjoy watching each other struggle? How does this compare to the way people treat each other vis-à-vis their primary treatment goals? Sometimes the group members on the outside will have difficulty watching their peers struggle, and they will offer more help than is requested. This dynamic has direct application to families in which a member may be struggling. Help that is sought tends to be valued much more readily than help that is imposed. The consequences in terms of this game are negligible, but when someone's self-destructive behavior is the subject, such as when a family member is abusing drugs or involved in another risky behavior, the consequences can be severe.

Source: LeFarve, 2002.

Pass a Sound and Gesture; One-Word Stories; Three-Headed Oracle

Materials Needed: None
Approximate Time: Varies
Description: These three activities come from a tradition of theatrical improvisation. They are designed to engender a sense of free expression and playfulness in your group members. While these qualities are obviously germane to acting, they are also useful in mental health treatment. We want the people we treat to express themselves as fully and spontaneously as possible, so these warm-up activities can be a means to free up expression. While the

content generated during the exercises tends to be silly, the process of free expression can lead to some deep therapeutic work.

Pass a Sound and Gesture is fairly self-explanatory. The group stands in a circle and someone makes eye contact with another member of the group and "passes" a sound and gesture to him or her. The person who "catches" the sound and gesture indicates this by repeating, to the best of their ability, the exact sound and gesture that was passed. They then pass a different sound and gesture combination to another member of the group, and the pattern repeats. This activity invites participants to reflect on how spontaneous or inhibited they feel.

From this you can move into One-Word Stories, in which each member of the group adds one word to form a story. Punctuation marks may be added in addition to a single word, but nothing more. The collective unconscious of the group often comes to light during these stories. It can be challenging for group members to add a simple article when that is what is needed to move the story along. People tend to want to exercise their creativity rather than add a connector such as "an" or "the" that might support the story as a whole. Use this as an opportunity to talk about individual versus collective efforts. See if the story can hold together, and allow the story to reach its natural conclusion.

The last improv activity in the sequence is called Three-Headed Oracle. This is a variation on One-Word Story, described above, except that this time only three people participate at a time. Three members of the group form the all-knowing oracle by standing or sitting side by side. Another member of the group asks the Three-Headed Oracle a question, and the question is answered in the same manner that the One-Word Story was told: with each of the three "heads" adding just one word at a time to form the answer. This tends to be a lot of fun and provides a nice follow-up to the prior activity, which was more inclusive of the whole group. This one is self-selecting. If you have a group in which everyone wants to be part of an oracle, you can play several rounds with different oracles fielding the questions. Allow those on the sidelines to generate the questions for the oracles.

Processing Points: What nonverbal cues did people communicate during the initial warm-up? If some emotional content seems apparent, the therapist can highlight this or provide an opportunity for reflection. However, the process of free expression is the main point of passing sounds and gestures. You might ask how people felt during this activity. Unless you have former or current actors in your group, people are likely to feel self-conscious at the idea of looking silly in front of their peers. This notion is definitely worth delving into as self-consciousness is the bane of many therapy patients' lives.

For One-Word Stories and Three-Headed Oracle, you can ask if people were able to "stay in the moment" and not try to plan ahead. Being fully present is difficult for most of us and is a key tenet of DBT and mindfulness, two popular approaches to therapy. It's seemingly impossible to think about the future and listen carefully to what is being said at the same moment. How can we learn to trust ourselves to think of the right thing to say when the moment comes and in doing so dedicate ourselves fully to the task of listening? It seems that the process of giving our undivided attention to others could be invaluable in many situations. What are some of these? What got in people's way of giving their full attention to listening? What gets in the way in other settings?

Source: Spolin, 1983.

Word Circles

Materials Needed: Index cards or strips with one word printed on each card or strip. You can create your own word circles or use ones generated by Chris Cavert on his blog www.fundoing.com/blog.

Approximate Time: 10 minutes. People seem to enjoy this challenge and they are usually willing to solve two or three of them, time permitting.

Description: Word circles are puzzles that are solved by the group. Each person in the group receives a word, assuming that you have a word circle set that matches the number of group members. If not, you can assign one or two people to observe or assist, or two people can represent a single word. The challenge for the group members is to position themselves so that each two-word phrase makes sense; that is, each word needs to work with the ones just before and after it so that a chain of compound words or phrases is formed. Each group member must hold his or her word throughout the activity. You can play it on a tabletop, but that is not as much fun, nor is it as physically engaging. For the purposes of illustration, let's say you were working with a small group of six, and the words used were "back," "cage," "door," "pack," "rat," and "way." How can you arrange all six words so that all of the pairs make sense? One solution might be "back-pack-rat-cage-door-way" (and the circle connects "back" to the beginning!).

Processing Points: How did the group go about solving the puzzle? Was it useful to have people offer different perspectives, or did one person more or less take over the problem-solving? Could the problem-solving method be improved upon over time? If multiple perspectives were helpful, where else is this true? Many times, members of therapeutic groups benefit from having others offer an alternative perspective of them. Often others can see our best qualities better than we can see them ourselves.

The Funnies

Materials Needed: Enlarged copies of single-panel comics with the captions removed. The captions should be typed in large print and cut into strips.

Cartoons from the *New Yorker* work particularly well for this activity, but one-panel cartoons from newspapers or other sources are fine too. Allow at least one caption and drawing per group member.

Approximate Time: 10 minutes

Description: Lay all the enlarged comics out on a table. You might want to laminate these if you plan to use them again. Give each group member a caption. It's okay if you have more comics than group members: that just makes it a bit more challenging. Explain that the task is for the group to match each caption with its comic. You will let the group know whether or not they have been successful after they are through, but in the event that they are not successful, you will only tell them that much and not specifically which of the captions are misplaced. You can also explore the idea that there might be more than one "right" solution even though there is only one solution that is consistent with the source material. If the group members can "see" another combination that makes sense, that is satisfactory and a great opportunity to talk about subjectivity. It then becomes the group's job to continue to attempt to solve the puzzle. This is where it becomes more of a group activity. Usually for the first go-round, each person is looking to match his or her own caption. During ensuing rounds, more of the group members will be engaged in looking at the puzzle as a whole.

Processing Points: You might want to explore with your group members to what extent this was an individual activity versus a group challenge. How did people respond after they had placed their own caption? Did they feel as if their part was done and become disengaged, or did that free them up to assist others? What kinds of relationships emerged between group members during the activity? Were they cooperative or competitive? Did some group members remain more involved than others, and if so, why?

The "correct answers" to this puzzle are somewhat subjective. Usually, the best answers will be the ones that were originally part of the comics, but there are instances in which more than one caption could arguably make sense. Feel free to be flexible with this and use it as an opportunity to discuss varying points of view. Conflicting points of view are generally at the root of much discord in the world. Ask your group members to reflect on times that they have become entrenched in a disagreement with a family member, a colleague, or a friend. What made it hard to see the other person's point of view? If you include psychodrama in your programming and the discussion generates fitting material, feel free to branch off into a psychodrama session at this point, or note the material for later use. For a description of psychodrama, see chapter 18 of this book or consult Dayton (2010) or Yablonsky (1976).

Scrabble

Materials Needed: A "team-building" Scrabble set. This can be made by using a marker to write individual letters on whatever material you are using (index cards, old tennis balls, slices of a foam pool noodle, or any other viable material) so that you end up with a complete Scrabble-like set. I use old tennis balls and keep them in a plastic crate. You would think that they would roll around when placed on the ground, but they tend to stay in place, even on hard floors.

Approximate Time: 20 minutes

Description: Divide your group into teams of six each. Start with a few rounds of four-, five-, and six-letter-word warm-ups. Ask each group member to pick a letter out of the box or bag. Each small group is challenged to create a word using any four of their six letters. Each person must hold his or her own letter throughout. If no word can be formed, one or more people from the group is elected to exchange his or her letter for a new one. Once a word is formed, it should be displayed to the rest of the group. Each person stands in order, holding his or her letter facing outward. People whose letters are not being used take the point of view of the larger group and help their small group organize itself to display the word. Once each of the small groups has been successful in spelling a four-letter word, have everyone exchange their letters for new ones and repeat the activity using five- and then six-letter words.

After these warm-up rounds are finished, explain that the next challenge is for everyone to play a Scrabble-like game in which a crossword puzzle is created in the middle of the playing area. Whichever group can create a six-letter word first begins by placing their word in the middle. Then each person from that small group takes a new letter. The next small group builds a word onto the first word using general Scrabble guidelines (all contiguous letters must form words, no proper nouns, etc.), *but* feel free to add additional guidelines or to forgo the "no proper nouns" rule. For example, you could say that all words have to be related to mental health and recovery. Keep playing until all the letters have been used or cannot be played. Since no scorekeeping is done, there is no reason why the small groups can't combine their resources to form the last few words. This brings the large group back together.

Processing Points: What memories were stimulated by playing this game? Do you have happy or stressful memories of playing Scrabble? How was this version different from the one you remember? There are two striking differences. One is that this version is physical. It can even be aerobic if enough distance lies between the teams and the "board." How do your group members generally feel about being physically active? In which instance are they more comfortable, and how has this impacted them in school, at work, and with their families? The other obvious difference is that this version is played in small groups as opposed to individually. How did that part of the experience compare for your group members? In which instance do they feel more comfortable, and if so, why? Are there other times when they might prefer to engage in a challenge using the support of a group? Explore these. You might want to loosen the rules of Scrabble for young adults or adolescents so that proper nouns and slang words are acceptable. This will accentuate inclusiveness and collaboration and deemphasize perfectionism.

Group Scrabble. *Photo by the author.*

Chapter Nine

Paper Day

Beyond Reading and Writing on Paper

Paper is ubiquitous in our society even as we are moving to so-called paper-less systems. We write papers through our many years of formal education, we get receipts when we shop, we continually sign contracts, disclaimers, and related agreements, and the list goes on. Most of us are bogged down with more paperwork than we can reasonably process. But what happens when a simple 8½×11-inch sheet of paper is used as a source of play? The meta-communication that says, "Paper can be a source of fun" is in itself a tacit, cognitive intervention. Most psychiatric patients (and professionals!) come to associate paper with prescriptions for medication and a seemingly endless series of assessments, treatment plans, and HIPAA forms. The series of activities that follow offers a subtle antidote to the weight of so much paperwork as the very same materials are used for playfulness and immediate self-discovery. Please recycle!

QUESTION OF THE DAY

What uses can you think of for paper other than writing on? This question opens the door to an awareness that paper can be and is used for many different purposes. Think of paper airplanes and origami, tinder for building fires, confetti, the base of many art forms, etc.

PAPER DAY ACTIVITIES

Paper Drop

Materials Needed: One 8½×11-inch sheet of paper
Approximate Time: 10 minutes
Description: This name game offers an array of metaphorical associations and is in itself an engaging way to begin a session. Ask your group members to stand in a circle. If people are not acquainted with each other's names, have everyone introduce themselves. Then explain that one person will start in the middle of the circle. He will hold a sheet of paper above his head and call out another group member's name as he releases the sheet of paper. The person whose name was called tries to catch the paper before it falls to the ground. The person who dropped the paper steps out of the way so as not to interfere with the attempt. If the person whose name was called is successful in catching the sheet of paper before it hits the ground, he or she repeats the sequence by calling another group member's name as the paper is released. If the paper hits the floor before being caught, the person in the middle rips the piece of paper in half, puts half of the sheet in his or her pocket, and drops the remaining half sheet of paper while calling another group member's name. A standard piece of paper can be halved about eight to 10 times before it becomes impossible to work with.

Processing Points: What did the sheet of paper represent? Was there a silver lining to missing a catch (the person ends up owning part of a resource)? If the resource has value, then there certainly was a benefit in not having caught it. Is this like anything else in life when not succeeding at something results in getting something of value? Some people who are involved in 12 Step recovery refer to themselves as "grateful" recovering addicts. Their gratitude is usually due to the idea that their recovery has offered them much more than freedom from an addiction. It has often provided a supportive community as well as guideposts to living. In that sense, having "failed" at drinking as a normal person resulted in something of value: a new way of life. Are there other analogies you can think of?

Was the paper easier or more difficult to catch as it decreased in size? Where else in life are things more manageable as they decrease in size? Where does the aphorism "Less is more" come into play? If the larger paper was easier to catch, then we might reflect on what resources we really value and want to protect. There are many directions you can go with the processing of this one. Did some people's names seem to get called more often than others? Where else does this happen and why do things work out this way?

Source: Michael Gass at an AEE conference.

Paper Drop. *Photo by the author.*

Paper Towers

Materials Needed: A stack of 8½×11-inch paper. Feel free to recycle paper that has been used for other purposes.

Approximate Time: 15 minutes

Description: Divide your group into smaller groups of three to four people each. Give each group 12–20 sheets of paper and explain that they have 10 minutes to build the tallest free-standing structure they can using only the sheets of paper they have been given. After 10 minutes, comparisons will be made by the group leader. The group with the tallest tower that can remain free-standing for at least 30 seconds "wins." This activity can be done on tabletops or starting from the floor, depending upon the needs of your group members and available space. To enrich the metaphorical application of this activity, ask your group members to write the name of a recovery-oriented resource on each of the sheets of paper before construction of the towers begins.

Processing Points: Explore the ways in which each group went about the task and also the relationship that emerged between the various small groups. Was the atmosphere competitive or cooperative? The activity is set up as a competition. How did that impact the way group members felt about the other groups? Were design concepts handled as if they were proprietary or to be freely exchanged between the groups? Where else in life do these dynamics appear? Why are we so focused on individual achievement in our society? The aphorism "Imitation is the sincerest form of flattery" may be relevant here.

What about the dynamics that emerged within each small group? If you were working with co-leaders, was there an opportunity for each group to have its own staff member observing? Did group members remain in their typical role of leader or follower? How does this work for them in various situations, and in what ways would they like to grow?

You can also discuss the tradeoff between stability and design. Was each small group more focused on looking good and coming out ahead, or did they try to erect a structure that was built to last? There may be analogies here to the way each individual is going about the treatment process. Are they working to maintain a secure base that they can build on or do they just want to complete the process and move on with their lives?

Source: Karl Rohnke at a TEAM conference.

Paper Doorway

Materials Needed: One or two 8½×11-inch sheets of paper and a pair of scissors

Approximate Time: 20–30 minutes

Description: Give the group one 8½×11-inch sheet of paper and a pair of scissors. I keep a second sheet on hand and consider giving it upon request, if needed. Most groups can solve the challenge using just one sheet. The objective is for the group to keep the paper as a continuous piece but cut in such a way that each member of the group can pass through the sheet, meaning that their entire body passes from one side of the sheet to the other. The piece of paper must not be taped or tied in any way. Note that there are very limited resources to work with so time must be taken to plan carefully before executing any idea that is agreed upon. Some groups need to discover this experientially.

Processing Points: Where else are scarce resources an issue? Did the group move into action before it was really ready to? How did the group work together to solve the problem? Did certain people emerge as leaders? Did some people have ideas that they were afraid to express, or did some ideas get expressed that were not listened to? This activity can be very frustrating, so it offers a good opportunity to explore low frustration tolerance. When would group members benefit from having an expanded ability to tolerate frustration?

Paper Doorway. *Photo by the author.*

Traffic Jam

Materials Needed: One more sheet of paper than there are group members; for example, 11 sheets of paper for a group of 10

Approximate Time: 20 minutes

Description: This activity requires an even number of players. If there is an odd number in your group, offer an opportunity for one person to act as an observer. They could become very helpful to the group! To start, place all the pieces of paper on the floor in a row, about two feet apart, and have each group member stand on a piece of paper, with one blank piece in the middle (see diagram below for starting and ending positions). When in the starting position, every group member should be facing the blank sheet in the middle. The challenge is for both subgroups (one facing each way) to end up on the opposite side of the blank sheet in the middle. Group members can only move according to the following criteria:

1. A group member may step onto a blank sheet that is directly in front of him or her.
2. A group member may pass one person who is facing opposite them to step onto a blank spot.
3. A person *may not pass* someone who is facing the same way they are.
4. Once a group member has taken a step forward, they may not backtrack. If a traffic jam occurs (if the group cannot progress according the guidelines above), the group starts over.

Processing Points: This activity emphasizes perspective. With all group members standing in a straight line, it becomes very difficult for any one group member to maintain perspective of the whole group. That is why it might be useful to have an outside observer who is available to make suggestions. In what other instances have your group members been unable to gain perspective in a difficult situation? When someone is struggling in school or at work, they may not be able to see that the knowledge and experience that

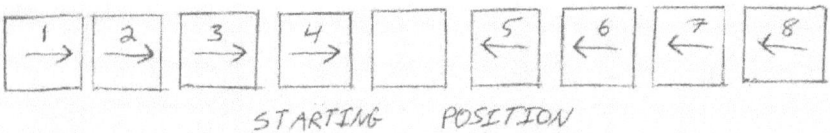

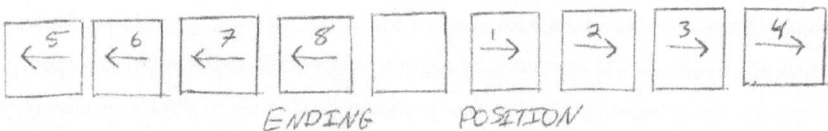

Traffic Jam starting and ending positions. *Created by the author.*

they gain from the struggle will pay dividends in unexpected ways. For example, I worked with a participant who had an extremely difficult time tolerating and then withdrawing from psychiatric medications. She subsequently became an advocate for others who were struggling in similar ways. There is no way she could have known at the time that her difficulties would make her an asset to others because she lacked the perspective of time. Whenever a person is part of a large system that they cannot see in its entirety, blocks in perspective may occur. We get a limited and rosy picture of other people's lives based on their Facebook profiles, for example, and this limited perspective prevents us from really understanding their circumstances. Discuss with your group ways in which gaining perspective has helped people manage a challenging situation.

Note: Activities such as Key Punch (chapter 10) and Stepping Stones (chapter 13) can be done using paper as the primary material.

Chapter Ten

Numbers Day

Multiply Your Strengths

Most of us associate numbers with math class, financial matters, and score-keeping, but numbers can also be used in more whimsical ways, as in the activities described in this chapter. Numbers can reflect progress made toward treatment goals, or for those working a 12 Step program, the numbered steps offer a specific trajectory for personal growth. And just as words became toys in chapter 8, numbers too can be used as objects of play rather than merely as markers of scores or yard lines.

QUESTION OF THE DAY

What scales do you use for self-reflection or self-assessment or time-management purposes?

Psychological tests are full of Likert scales and other numerical values assigned to people's moods and overall functioning. Many of us have internalized such ways of ranking our mood or our sense of enjoyment or the importance of items on our "To do" lists. We use numbers and scales as a way of organizing our thoughts and our priorities. Ask your group members to share with each other what quantitative measures they employ on a daily basis. You can then discuss the overall impact of the measurements and allow people to make suggestions to one another in the event that the scales are being used for self-criticism as opposed to self-improvement.

NUMBER DAY ACTIVITIES

Substitute Counting

Materials Needed: None
Approximate Time: 5 minutes
Description: Group members work in pairs for this warm-up activity. Begin by asking each pair to count to three repeatedly, with each person alternating numbers. For example, the person who says "One" and "Three" the first time through says "Two" the second time through, and so on and so forth, as follows:

Person A: "One"
Person B: "Two"
Person A: "Three"
Person B: "One"
Person: A: "Two"
Person B: "Three"

The pattern then repeats.

Allow each pair to get comfortable counting this way. Next, explain that sounds and movements will now be substituted for the numbers. You can make up any combination of alternatives to the numbers. Some of the ones I have used are stomping a foot, snapping a finger, clapping, or popping one's lips. Assign a sound and movement to each of the numbers, and ask each pair to repeat the counting pattern, this time using the sounds and alternate movements instead of the numbers. Allow enough time for your group members to grow comfortable practicing this new language.

Processing Points: What was required in order to achieve success during this activity? Most people will say that they had to remain "in the moment," focused solely on the task at hand. Was having such focus therapeutic? Did it hold other preoccupations at bay, at least temporarily? What was is like to try something new? Was this anxiety-provoking for some people? Where else do new situations create anxiety? Think of the first day at a new job or starting a new training program or class. Did group members evaluate themselves or just allow themselves to try their best? Where else does this dynamic come into play?

Source: Spolin, 1983.

Six Count

Materials Needed: None
Approximate Time: 5 minutes

Description: The dynamics of this routine are similar to Substitute Counting except the group leader teaches the sequence to the whole group at once and each person works on his or her own and learns the pattern. Demonstrate a "six count" with your right arm so that your arm is raised overhead on each odd number and down by your side with each even number. Ask the group to repeat the pattern with you: "One" (up), "Two" (down), "Three" (up), "Four" (down), "Five" (up), and "Six" (down). Now, using the opposite arm, demonstrate a different six-count. This time the left arm goes overhead on "One" but rather than coming all the way back down on "Two," the arm extends straight out from the shoulder to the side on "Two," and then all the way back down on "Three." Repeat the sequence so that the arm goes up overhead on "Four," sideways on "Five," and all the way down on "Six." Have the group members repeat and master this sequence. The challenge is to do both patterns at once, so that each arm is in a different position on all the numbers except "One and "Six."

Processing Points: Like Substitute Counting, this activity focuses on adaptability and willingness to try something new. Changing habits takes time, practice, and patience. Did the way people went about learning Six Count reveal any obstacles they might be encountering in their therapeutic goals?

Sum Totals

Materials Needed: None
Time: 5 minutes
Description: Start in pairs. Ask each person in each pair to use one hand and on a count of three extend one to five fingers. Keep going until the sum total of all fingers equals seven. Next, work in groups of three, and keep going until the sum equals 11; next try groups of four until a sum of 14 is reached, and continue to groups of five until a sum of 17 is reached.

Processing Points: The only real difficulty this activity presents is being spontaneous when working with different groups of people. This is a nice opportunity to discuss the Serenity Prayer, if the people you are working with use it, which helps people distinguish between things that are within their control and things that are not. In this case, each person can only be responsible for the number of fingers they contribute to the total. What does it feel like to have to live with the consequences of other people's choices? In this activity, the consequences are not meaningful, but in life, what kinds of issues emerge when someone else's behavior does not align with our own vision of how things should be done? Where does this get us into trouble, and under what circumstances are we willing to change in order to accommodate others?

Zing

Materials Needed: None

Approximate Time: 5–10 minutes

Description: This counting game is often referred to as "Buzz" when it is used as a drinking game, but since many of the people we work with have had problems abusing alcohol or other drugs, I prefer to use a different word, in this case, "zing." The group counts out loud in sequence around a circle. The first time through, if a number either has "five" in it, or is a multiple of 5, the word "zing" is said in place of the number. This round is relatively easy since each multiple of 5 ends in either 0 or 5. Next try using 7 as the variable. This is considerably more difficult, since multiples of 7 end in various numbers and do not have the consistent pattern that multiples of 5 have.

Processing Points: This is another activity that supports a mindfulness approach to mental health treatment. If we can stay focused on what is right in front of us, we will probably be less disturbed by other preoccupying thoughts. What are some situations in which group members tend to get preoccupied thinking about what might happen next as opposed to staying focused on the present moment? Any time people are motivated by a particular outcome, preoccupying thoughts can interfere with the experience. Job interviews, sporting competitions, and dating come to mind as three such instances. What other situations are relevant here?

Zen Counting

Materials Needed: None

Approximate Time: 5–10 minutes

Description: Group members should spread out randomly. Eyes can be open or closed. The challenge is for the group to count out loud from 1 to 20, in a random pattern, with each group member saying at least one number. If a number is said simultaneously by two or more people, the group must start again from 1. No advance planning is allowed. You can also use the alphabet as a variation.

Processing Points: Sometimes less is more. In many instances, the greatest contribution a group member can make is to stay out of the way (which in this case means remaining silent after they have said at least one number). Also, a slower pace can lead to greater success in this challenge. Where else does this apply? How did the way people listened to each other evolve as the group made multiple attempts? Does the quality with which we listen to each other change as well? How so?

Key Punch

Materials Needed: Spot markers numbered 1 to 20 and enough rope or other material to make a large square, say about 10 x 10 feet, plus another strip of material to form a starting line. The spot markers can be made from old CDs with numbers written on them with a black marker, rubber discs, ovals cut from cabinet lining material, or even pieces of paper.

Approximate Time: 20 minutes

Description: Scatter the numbers randomly within the roped-off area. There are a few different variations of this activity so please feel free to experiment with them and adapt the activity to suit your group's needs. All the variations involve group members finding and stepping on numbers in sequence.

Variation 1: In the first variation, I ask the group to stand behind the starting line about thirty feet from the numbers. I explain that this is a timed event, and the challenge is for the group to move to the numbers and count them off in sequence (1 to 20, for example) while each number is stepped on in sequence. Each person in the group must touch and say at least one number. The group members must then return to behind the starting line. Usually group members will feel disoriented during the first attempt, as they don't know where the numbers are positioned, and they are trying something for the first time, plus the directions may sound ambiguous. Based on the time of the preliminary attempt, a goal of a reduced time is established, and the group has several chances to attempt it.

Processing Points: What is it like to be trying something without completely understanding what is expected of you? Have you ever encountered a situation like this before? In what ways did the group go about improving its time on subsequent attempts? Did leaders emerge within the group?

Variation 2: In this variation, all the members of the group stand around the roped-off field of numbers. This time, rather than have each person count one or two numbers, every person must run the full sequence of numbers, and a timed goal for the whole group is established. This is usually done by having one person test-drive the course, i.e., run the numbers, stepping on each number, 1 to 20, in sequence. The facilitator times this attempt, and based on this and the number of group members participating, a timed group goal is established. The agreed-upon goal is usually somewhat less than what the direct multiple would be because we can assume that people going later will have benefited from having seen others go through the sequence and will therefore be able to attain a better time. For example, if the test runner times in at 20 seconds and there are nine group members, a goal of nine times 20 seconds would be 180 seconds, or three minutes. We might therefore suggest a goal of 2½ minutes for such a group, assuming that the times would likely get better as group members observed those who had gone before them. This

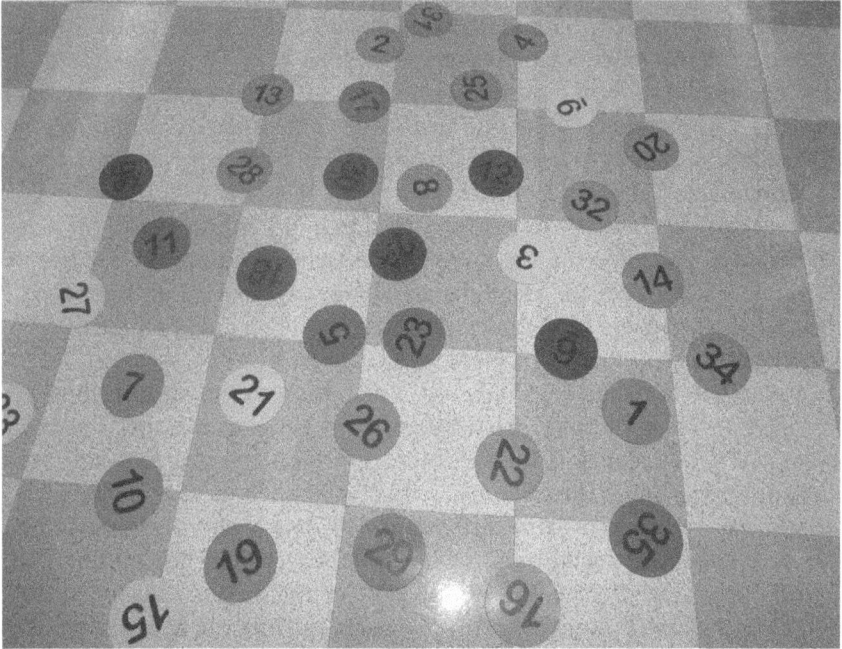

Key Punch setup. *Photo by the author.*

variation invites those on the outside to encourage and support the person running the numbers.

Processing Points: How would you describe the quality of support that those on the outside gave to the people in the middle? Was it the right amount of support, or too much or too little? Were people able to request the level of support that they needed, or was this imposed on them? This is relevant to other areas in life. Talk about the difference between support that is requested and support that is foisted upon someone.

Invite your group members to reflect on the difference between supporting others from the outside of the playing area and being the one in action trying to find their way through the sequence. Most of us find it easier to offer support to others than to take it in. Were group members exclusively supportive while they stood on the perimeter, or did they also judge one another? In what other settings do we need to choose between being supportive or judgmental of others who might be struggling? In treatment settings, there will invariably be people who are struggling to stay on course. Do we judge such people as lazy or insincere or do we support them in trying to do better next time?

Finally, the process of learning from others seems to have applications to the recovery process. What courses of action have we seen work well for others that we might like to try ourselves? Can we learn from others' mistakes? When someone who is in recovery relapses, they can be scorned ("You weren't careful enough with your plan") or appreciated ("I will use this as a lesson to avoid making the same missteps").

Chapter Eleven

Rope Day

Securing Success

Boaters and mountain climbers tend to be skilled at tying knots and otherwise working with rope. Others may associate rope with childhood activities such as tug-of-war, jump rope, and rope climbing. Rope lengths of various sizes can also be used as the basis for a number of problem-solving challenges. Some of them are presented here.

QUESTION OF THE DAY

We Americans are dog lovers. Some of our canine friends need to be kept on a leash at all times while others are permitted to roam freely, their owners trusting that they won't run away. Metaphorically speaking, we use the expression "Being kept on a short leash" to mean that we are highly accountable to someone (usually someone who has authority over us), and it also implies limitations being placed on us, often for our own well-being. In what ways are we "kept on a short leash" or given room to roam? Whom are we accountable to? Would we like to have greater autonomy, and what might we do with such freedom once we had it? Do we want to have a "longer leash" or are we grateful to those who are looking out for our safety?

ROPE DAY ACTIVITIES

Fast Pitch

Materials Needed: One 3-foot piece of paracord or other rope that is about ⅛ of an inch in diameter and tied into a loop for each group member. These rope circles will be used as spot markers. One easily catchable ball is also needed.

Approximate Time: 20 minutes

Description: This is a variation of the group juggling activity described in chapter 7. To set up the activity, make a large circle out of the rope loops. Each group member should stand in one of the rope loops so that they are about an arm's length from the people to their immediate right and left. Ask your group members to toss the ball to each person in a random order without getting it to any one person twice. The person tossing the ball should say the name of the intended recipient, so this initial round can function as a refresher of people's names for newer groups. The ball should end up with the person who began the cycle. The challenge grows from here.

After the group has completed the first task, explain that you would like them to try it again, except this time everyone should move to the circle of the person they have thrown the ball to after that person has caught the ball. In other words, each person should end up inside the circle of the person they tossed the ball to.

Groups often end up with one person displaced as they find themselves stuck in an infinite loop, with one person continually being displaced. Allow the group to struggle for as long as seems tolerable before you start providing hints that the key is to separate the two tasks. If the group starts by first getting the ball to each person and then *only after the full cycle is completed* moving to their new positions, they will be successful. Most group members get hung up on trying to move immediately after they have tossed the ball, as opposed to waiting until after each person has caught and tossed the ball, and only then moving in unison. Of course, the facilitator has helped to cause this confusion in the setup by saying, "You need to occupy the position of the person you have thrown the ball to after you make the pass." Many people will infer that "after" means "immediately after," which in this case it does not.

Processing Points: By combining a Name Game with a significant problem-solving activity, you stand the risk of plunging the group into a difficult challenge before they have had time to grow comfortable with one another. This activity offers opportunities to talk about what roles may be emerging in the group as well as what feelings arose for the participants. When do we make assumptions as opposed to really thinking about what might be conducive to success?

Source: Cavert, 2015.

Hup-Two-Three-Four

Materials Needed: One length of rope 20–30 feet long made into a large loop by tying the two ends together

Approximate Time: 10 minutes

Description: Place the large rope circle on the floor and ask your group members to march around the outside of the circle in unison, with one group member keeping the pace by repeatedly chanting aloud, "Hup, two, three, four" in synchrony with everyone's steps so that everyone is stepping with their right and left feet simultaneously. Once a coordinated pattern has been established, the group tries to switch to the inside of the rope, all at the same moment. After a couple of revolutions inside the rope, the group again switches to outside the rope, in time with the leader's cue. The designated leader can cue the switching by saying "Switch" instead of "Hup" every other cycle or with whatever timing the group decides on. I suggest setting a goal for the group of four to six synchronized switches, meaning that the group moves from inside to outside and back again, in unison, a set number of times without falling out of sync with each other.

Processing Points: This seemingly simple military-style drill is more challenging than it sounds. Why is it so difficult for a group to coordinate its efforts? What feelings come up for people when they are being asked to literally march in step? Does this directive stimulate resistance or even rebellion in some people? Which group members emerged in leadership roles, and why was this the case? You can use this question as a starting point for talking about leadership in other contexts.

Source: Karl Rohnke at a TEAM workshop.

Eight Pieces of Pie

Materials Needed: Four lengths of rope, one larger than the other three. The three shorter ropes should be approximately the length of the diameter of the longer rope once the larger rope has been made into a circle.

Approximate Time: 5 minutes

Description: Make the larger rope into a circle. Ask the group to arrange the three remaining rope pieces in such a way that the "pie" is cut into eight pieces. This problem-solving activity, along with the following two, is especially well suited to groups of three to six participants. The solution is counterintuitive because most people will think of making the pie into six pieces using the three ropes as in a pizza pie, but by crisscrossing two of the ropes and making a smaller circle inside the larger one with the remaining rope, the pie is divided into eight pieces.

Source: "Things to Do with Rope," Project Adventure.

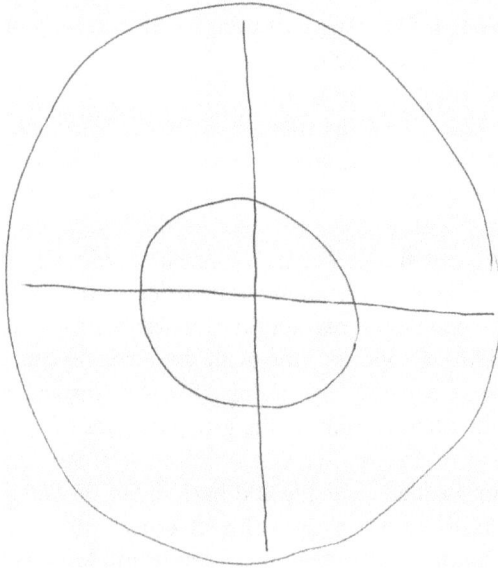

Dividing the pie in a unique way. *Created by the author.*

Not Knot

Materials Needed: One 20-foot length of ½-inch rope tied into several knots and then left in a loose clump on the floor. The challenge is for the group to guess how many knots have been tied, *without touching or moving the rope*. This task draws on the group members' observational skills as well as their collaborative abilities to bring their various perspectives together.

Spaghetti Junction

Materials Needed: Five roughly equivalent lengths of rope. Using rope lengths of different colors makes the task easier. Tie four of the rope lengths in a loop around the fifth rope loop, and as with Not Knot above, drop all five ropes together in a loose pile. Explain that one rope is being used to hold the other four together, as in a keychain. Can the group guess which rope is functioning as the "key-ring" for the other four?

Processing Points: The three preceding activities are all spatially oriented problem-solving challenges. Some people are more spatially aware than others, so those with such abilities may be pulled into leadership roles during this series of activities. What feelings arose in people as they engaged with an unfamiliar task? How did the group decide when to test their hypotheses? Was a consensus established? Were there people in the group who wanted to

Not Knot. *Photo by the author.*

take more time before "pulling the trigger?" How do we decide when it's time to move ahead with our plans or when further reflection is warranted?

Source: "Things to Do with Rope," Project Adventure.

Turnstile

Materials Needed: One length of rope long enough for playing jump rope with multiple participants

Approximate Time: 10 minutes

Description: This is a rather aerobic challenge for all involved. Ask two members of your group to hold either end of the rope, and have them start making giant swings in a continual circle so that other group members can take turns jumping the rope as they pass from one side to the other. The challenge is to get all the members of the group from one side of the rotating rope to the other in succession without interrupting the turning of the rope. To encourage role flexibility, ask people to cycle in and out of the rope-turning job. Can group members alternate the rope-turning positions while others are jumping through?

Processing Points: How did your group members respond to being in the supportive rope-turning role as opposed to jumping through? Which role was considered more valuable? Both were important, but was one considered to be of greater value? Obviously in business, managerial roles are valued over labor-focused roles, but what about in families? Is the "bread winner" valued more than the homemaker, or is the creative child valued more than their academically focused sibling, or vice versa?

Defining Personal Boundaries

Materials Needed: Several pieces of rope of varying length and thickness

Approximate Time: 15 minutes

Description: The flexible quality of rope provides a nice opportunity to allow group members to physically define and maintain their personal boundaries. Pat Ogden (2018) uses lengths of rope to help her patients talk about their boundaries. The participant encircles him- or herself in a piece of rope and the rope becomes a boundary through which others in the group need to gain permission before crossing. The individual who establishes the boundary can regulate it by granting or denying permission for others to cross it.

Processing Points: This isometric representation of personal boundaries can provide the basis for a discussion about other personal boundaries, such as how much of a person's time, attention, or other involvement they want to give to another person. How challenging or easy is it for group members to manage their own boundaries? What relationships are particularly challenging in this area, and in what ways would individuals like to gain greater ability to define and maintain their personal boundaries?

Source: Institute for Sensorimotor Psychotherapy.

Mergers

Materials Needed: At least as many rope circles as there are group members. The rope loops should be of various sizes, and placed in a random fashion on the floor. They can be made out of various lengths of paracord or any similar (⅛- to ¼-inch) type of rope.

Approximate Time: 10 minutes

Description: Explain that you would like each group member to stand so that no part of either foot is outside a rope circle. In other words, both feet need to be completely inside one or more of the rope loops on the floor. Now pick up any unused rope circles and say "Switch!" Each time the group hears you say "Switch," they should leave their current position and move to a new

Adjusting to diminishing resources. *Photo by Ben Silverman*

A solution. *Photo by Ben Silverman.*

one. While this transition is happening, you remove one of the rope circles, resulting in an ever diminishing space in which the group can work. Eventually, relying on each other to balance while standing will become untenable and the group will need to explore new options, such as sitting down and placing all of their feet in the loop of one rope. Once one person sits down, others invariably follow suit, with the group finding a relatively easy solution to what may have seemed out of reach just moments earlier. Following the lead of a good idea is a transferable process that can be used to address other issues, such as when a loved one begins to eat a healthier diet or exercise more regularly. Allow this solution to emerge from the group as opposed to providing it for them.

Processing Points: At what point do we decide that our current way of operating is no longer feasible? Why can it be so hard to make functional changes? This exercise allows a group to grapple with diminishing resources. The group adapts to the dwindling resources up to the point when a paradigm shift becomes necessary to accomplish the task.

This challenge also tests participants' threshold for personal proximity because group members tend to get very close physically during the later rounds. Was anyone's personal space compromised during the process? If so, why was it difficult to say so?

Source: "Things to Do with Rope," Project Adventure.

Chapter Twelve

Playing-Card Day

Everyone Wins

The traditional 52-card deck is often associated with games of chance and skill. The activities presented here open up a new range of possible uses for playing cards—among them are collaboration, problem-solving, role-playing, and real, unrestrained fun. The only prop required for the activities in this sequence is a deck of playing cards. You may wish to use an oversize or laminated deck for the novelty factor it offers and for ease of handling. Michelle Cummings (2007) has written a book containing over 50 team-building activities that can be done with a deck of cards. I refer readers who would like to expand on the few activities offered here to Cummings's book.

For some people, the 52-card deck may be associated with losing money because cards are often used for gambling. The activities presented here are all likely to have win-win outcomes.

QUESTION OF THE DAY

What is your favorite card game and can you recall an anecdote about playing it?

PLAYING-CARD DAY ACTIVITIES

Non-verbal Lineups

Materials Needed: A deck of playing cards
Approximate Time: 15 minutes

Description: This game can be played with anywhere from eight to 50 people, and it works especially well with medium-size groups of about 20.

Stage One: Shuffle the deck and hand a card to each group member. Ask your group members to refrain from looking at their own cards until after the task is completed. Instead, they should hold their card away from them, so that others can see their card, but they cannot. Next, explain that this is a non-verbal challenge; the goal is to complete the task without talking. Now ask the group to arrange itself in sequence, according to suit and numerical value, from lowest to highest. The group can decide whether the ace is high or low.

After the group is lined up, the facilitator should go through the line and determine whether or not they have been successful. If so, you can move on to the second challenge. If not, ask the group to try again, still without looking at their own cards.

Stage Two: After the group has completed the first task, ask the group members to rearrange themselves according to the alphabetical spelling of each card, from lowest (those beginning with *A*, such as the Ace of Clubs) to highest (the Two of Spades, for instance). The group may be disoriented by this direction. That's okay. Allow them to struggle as a group with comprehending the task. Again, after the group is lined up, determine whether or not they have been successful. If not, ask the group to keep trying. If so, allow people to look at their own cards and take some time to process the activity.

Processing Points: This series of activities can lead to some very rich discussion. One isometric metaphor concerns the parts of ourselves that others can see but that remain hidden to us. For example, sometimes others can read our emotions more easily than we can reflect on them ourselves. Can anyone think of times when this occurred, either when someone pointed something out to them that they had been previously unaware of or when they saw something in another person that they had not noticed in themselves?

Did some people in the group work harder than others at completing the task? Are these people prone to taking on more responsibility than is good for them? Did others hang back and if so, is this a familiar role for them? In what instances is doing so useful, and when does it interfere with one's goals? During the first lineup, did everyone agree upon how the suits were ordered and whether or not suits or digits got priority? In other words, did all the fours line up together and then sort themselves by suit, or did all the clubs line up together and then sort by digit? How did these decisions get made? How did the group decide whether the aces would be high or low? If someone saw things differently from the way the group worked it out, why did they choose to stay silent? You can then discuss what issues are worth engaging in conflict over and when it is best to go with the flow.

The movement created by the directions in the second lineup is worth reflecting upon because many of the high-value cards in the first lineup become low-value cards in the second lineup. The notable examples here are aces (if deemed high), twos, and threes. What real-life examples can you think of in which something of seemingly high value becomes devalued? Think of a marriage that ends in divorce or a high-priced stock that plummets. What if someone has a prized record or book collection but finds they need to move frequently? These possessions quickly become a burden. Are there other examples that you can think of?

Conversely, when does something seemingly insignificant increase in value? There are many examples of this: a previously unpublished manuscript becomes a best-seller and then is made into a successful movie; a small independent restaurant becomes a franchised operation; a person who is mandated to attend a 12 Step group becomes a leader within the organization; two strangers befriend each other, and so on. Allow your group members an opportunity to reflect on their own experiences to come up with additional examples.

Source: Cummings, 2007.

Play Your Card

Materials Needed: A deck of playing cards
Approximate Time: 20–30 minutes
Description: Begin with some warm-up exercises that invite heightened environmental and bodily awareness. Many of these come from a tradition of improvisational theater. For example, ask your group members to simply mill about the room, paying attention to things like their pace, posture, and which part of their body is leading them. Then you can suggest specific qualities that can inform their movement, such as weight (heaviness or lightness), pace (moving quickly or slowly), rhythm, etc. After a few minutes of practicing self-awareness, you can invite group members to begin noticing each other, maybe making brief eye contact and nonverbally acknowledging each other. You can then invite your group members to "shuttle" between self-awareness and awareness of the outside world.

After the group is sufficiently warmed up, explain that you are going to hand each person a card from the deck. They are not to show their card to anyone else. The value of the card will inform the way that each person continues moving and relating to others in the group; cards two through five denote very low status, whereas face cards and aces denote high status. Ask your group members to continue milling about, adjusting their posture, pace, and other movements to reflect the value of the card they were dealt. After giving people a minute to make adjustments, ask them to begin to interact nonverbally with each other. A simple acknowledgement, perhaps including eye contact and a gesture, as before, should be sufficient.

Allow enough time for each group member to interact with several other people. Then ask everyone to relax and begin a discussion including reactions and reflections on what people were able to observe during the exercise. It is a good idea to play at least two rounds so that your group members have experience exploring different roles.

Processing Points: This is potentially a very powerful activity and can unearth some strong feelings among your group members, especially those who have been oppressed or have lived with low self-esteem. If such an individual gets a low-value card, internalized devaluing projections might get stimulated. A highly narcissistic individual could run into similar difficulties if they receive a high-value card. The exaggerated sense of self that the individual has been contending with could get triggered. Before using this activity, it is important to think about the composition of your group. As a whole, and individually, are they prepared for a conversation that entails significant self-reflection, and can they handle the role-playing that this activity requires? If so, you may find that meaningful discussion unfolds as you ask your group members how it felt to play one role versus another. What kind of status do people ascribe to themselves? What qualities, in our society, contribute to having high status (some examples: a muscular figure, youthfulness, wealth) and what qualities contribute to the opposite (some examples: poverty, unattractiveness, involuntary unemployment)? How do people feel about the way that we, as a society, attribute value to some qualities and degrade other ones? Are there areas in which people have attained high status? A person in long-term recovery might be valued in the recovering community but not by larger society. What other subcultures can you think of in which the values differ from that of mainstream society? If you include a Joker in the cards that are distributed to your group members, you might get an impersonation of someone who is thought to be an outlier in society or of someone who plays by their own rules.

Zapper

Materials Needed: A deck of playing cards
Approximate Time: 10 minutes
Description: This game is often called Killer, but I have renamed it Zapper, because of the negative associations of the word "killer." Ask the members of your group to sit in a circle. Explain that the Queen of Diamonds (or whatever face card you choose) is the "zapper" card. Count out enough cards so that there is one per group member, and make sure that the zapper card is among them. Deal one card to each person. Explain that whoever receives the zapper card becomes the zapper for that round. His or her goal is to "zap" as many other people as possible without getting caught by subtly winking at other group members. Before dealing the cards, it's a good idea to

have people wink at each other for practice. Some people will need the practice and others will feel incompetent. Many people will giggle because winking tends to feel awkward.

The game is played simply by group members being available to each other through eye contact. All that is required is that people gaze at other group members around the circle. If someone gets winked at, they wait a few seconds and then pretend to faint. Encourage people to use their acting skills here; they should feel free to faint as dramatically or as subtly as they wish. The objective for others is to guess who the zapper is. If someone wants to guess, they should raise their hand. The facilitator calls on that person. If the guess is correct, the round is over. If the guess is wrong, the guesser closes their eyes and becomes one of the "zapped." After the zapper is discovered, do a quick count of the number of people they were able to zap before getting caught. This game tends to keep people engaged for five or more rounds. Keep track of the group record. It's quite challenging for most people to zap more than three or four without getting discovered.

Processing Points: Making eye contact can feel very vulnerable. What was it like for your group members to intentionally make eye contact with each other? What did it feel like to wink or be winked at? In what instances do people wink (some examples: to signal an inside joke, to signal approval, to indicate lecherous intentions)? The wink seems to have taken on lascivious connotations in recent years. Allow people to talk about this. Has the gesture fallen out of favor? What techniques did the zapper use? What methods did others use to try and figure out who the zapper was? Are these skills transferable or used in any other contexts? What other feelings were group members aware of as they played this game?

Source: Cummings, 2007.

New Deck

Materials Needed: A deck of playing cards and a stopwatch
Approximate Time: 10 minutes
Description: This is a variation of the facetious game 52 Pick Up. Scatter a deck of playing cards face-up on the floor. Explain that this is a timed challenge during which the group must arrange all the cards as if they were a brand-new deck so that all the cards are ordered both by suit and numerically. Allow the group to attempt this a first time through, and tell them their time. Next, explain that the group will attempt to improve its process and beat its former time. If you want to set a specific goal, feel free to do so. Most groups will be able to reduce their initial time by 25–50%. Scatter the cards again, and ask the group to once again deliver a "new" deck of cards.

Processing Points: What changed from the first attempt to the second? Why was it so much easier on subsequent attempts? What else grows easier with time and experience? What roles did group members take on during the activity? Are these familiar to them? When do these roles come in handy and when do they cause difficulties?

Chapter Thirteen

Tarp Day

An Indoor Adventure

A 6×8-foot plastic tarp is most readily associated with camping, as when it is used under a tent to prevent water and dirt from damaging the tent, or in situations in which paint or other messy work is being done. But a simple 6×8-foot plastic tarp can also be used for many team-building activities. Some of my favorites follow. Please note that not all the activities in this sequence use tarps; some are more loosely associated with the outdoors and camping. For example, a tent pole is the primary prop in the Helium Pole activity, and plastic drinking cups are used in two other challenges. Cavert and Thompson (2017) have written a whole book about activities that involve cups. I refer those who would like to develop a Cup Day agenda to their book.

QUESTION OF THE DAY

If you were a body of water, what would you be and why? The possibilities are really limitless here (brooks, rivers, streams, bays, pools, bath tubs, etc.). This question gets people thinking metaphorically about themselves, invites them to share this with others, and subtly suggests that an enhanced self-concept is within reach.

TARP DAY ACTIVITIES

Tarp Turn

Materials Needed: One 6×8-foot plastic tarp
Approximate Time: 10–15 minutes
Description: Lay the tarp flat on the floor and ask everyone in your group to stand on it with both feet. Some tarps have a different color on one side than the other and it is useful, but not mandatory, to use a tarp like this. Explain that the task is for the group members to flip the tarp over *without stepping off it.* That is, no one may step on the floor or ground during the activity. Notify the group that you will ask them to start over if that happens. This activity requires your group members to be in very close proximity to one another, so use your discretion. The more people on the tarp, the more difficult the challenge. For groups larger than 12 or 15, you may want to use a second tarp and divide the group into two smaller groups.

Processing Points: Was this frustrating for people? How so? What was it like to endure some physical awkwardness? Was the close proximity uncomfortable? How so? If it felt unsafe in some way, were group members able to take care of themselves by setting appropriate boundaries? Roles can be discussed here as well.

I use this activity as a metaphor for Step 8 of AA's 12 Steps in that people are collectively turning a page and becoming willing to make amends to those they may have hurt in the past. I ask each group member to write the initials of someone they have hurt on a strip of masking tape. All the initialed strips of tape are then affixed to one side of the tarp and the side with the tape on it is placed face down at the beginning of the activity so that in flipping the tarp over, the group collectively indicates its readiness to look at the list of people they have harmed. This activity can be used as metaphor for any kind of change as represented by the phrase "Turning over a new leaf."

Holy Tarp

Materials Needed: One 6×8-foot tarp with five or more holes cut in it and some balls of various sizes and materials
Approximate Time: 20 minutes
Description: The tarp used should have five or more holes of various sizes cut in it. If using five holes, the pattern of five pips on a die can be used. The holes can vary in size somewhat. I suggest making most of the holes about 6 inches in diameter, with some holes slightly larger and a couple of smaller ones.

Ask the members of your group to hold the tarp as if they were spreading out a sheet. Up to 10 people can comfortably work with a 6×8-foot tarp.

Collectively turning over a new leaf. *Photo by Ben Silverman.*

Adjust the tarp size according to the size of your group. Explain that the task is for the group to move a ball around the circumference of all the holes without letting the ball fall through one of the holes or roll off the tarp. Group members can only hold the edges of the tarp. They cannot touch the ball directly but must manipulate the tarp to move the ball. If the ball falls through or off the tarp, you will ask the group to start over. Allow the group to select from and try using a variety of different balls. Generally, the smaller the ball, the greater the difficulty.

Processing Points: This activity lends itself beautifully to metaphorical application. What are the traps that can set us back in life? These traps are represented by the various holes in the tarp. Allow each hole to be imbued with the quality of a specific trap by members of your group. Some examples of traps could be hanging out with friends who are using drugs, all-or-nothing thinking, social isolation, and so on. It's important that the group members generate the suggestions so that the activity takes on meaning for them.

What do the various balls represent? What makes some balls more vulnerable to falling into a trap than others? What kinds of things can we do to steel ourselves against potential traps? How can we make ourselves less vulnerable to falling off our course of recovery? How did group members work together to achieve success during this activity? How was the process

Avoiding falling into traps. *Photo by Ben Silverman.*

similar to or different from the way people support one another in their therapeutic goals? In what ways was there room for improvement?

> This is a very challenging activity and groups tend to get frustrated as the balls fall repeatedly though the holes. I have seen group members become creative in these moments by ducking under the tarp and blocking one or more of the holes with their heads, from the bottom up! This comic attempt to address a challenging situation can generate laughter or annoyance from the other group members. This first time I saw group members do this, I had to decide whether I would view the behavior as cheating or as a creative attempt to help the group succeed. I opted for the latter and asked the group what it might mean for them to "block" negative self-talk or putting oneself in vulnerable situations.

Source: Cavert, 2015.

Helium Pole

Materials Needed: One tent pole, fully extended. The lighter the pole, the harder the challenge.
Approximate Time: 15 minutes
Description: Ask your group members to form two equal lines so that each person is facing someone in the opposite line and about four feet away.

Easy does it in recovery. *Photo by the author.*

Ask each person to extend a hand straight across to their partner, with their index finger extended. Place the tent pole horizontally so that it is resting on the tips of each person's index finger. Explain that the group's task is to lower the pole to the ground while maintaining contact with it at all times. If any member of the group loses contact with the pole, you will ask the group to start again. The more people involved, the more difficult the task becomes. The "helium stick" seems to magically float upward in spite of each group member's wish to bring it down. You might want to modify the guidelines depending on your group's threshold for frustration.

Processing Points: Things are not as easy as they seem. What other tasks seem as if they would be relatively easy but when attempted are actually quite challenging? What adjustments were required of the group in order to be successful here? Usually, slowing down is important. Where else would your group members benefit from slowing down? Was low frustration tolerance an issue during this activity? It often is. In AA and other 12 Step programs, the phrase "Easy does it" is used to suggest a state of mind that is conducive to long-term sobriety. The phrase seems to apply to this challenge too. You can't muscle the pole down. "Easy does it."

Sometimes a group member will try to control others in the group. This usually proves futile. The maxim "Less is more" may be applicable here.

Stepping Stones (aka River Crossing)

Materials Needed: One spot marker for each group member plus some way to indicate two banks of a river. Please note that a variety of materials can be used as spot markers. Rubber discs about one foot in diameter work well, as do square carpet samples that can be gotten from carpet stores that may be discarding last year's patterns. I like using foam pads because they raise people a little higher off the ground and add a sense of novelty to the challenge. Outdoor challenge courses often use slices of a tree trunk, though these are difficult to transport for portable programs. Masking tape and a few markers are optional.

Approximate Time: 20 minutes

Description: This classic team-building activity involves everyone in the group moving from one bank of an imaginary river to the other using only the spot markers they have been given. The group members must maintain contact with these markers, or "resources," at all times or they may lose them. Indicate the bank of the river on which the group will begin its journey. Allow about four feet per group member to measure the length of the crossing, and indicate the other bank of the river using a piece of rope, two chairs, a line in the dirt, etc. The other bank of the river represents the realization of their therapeutic goals. Ask each group member to imbue their marker with a resource they want to take with them on their journey. A resource can be anything that supports their recovery (e.g., meditation, thought-stopping techniques, exercise, etc.). Optionally, you can ask your group members to write the name of their resource on a piece of tape that they can then apply to their spot marker.

Staying connected with our resources. *Photo by the author.*

Explain that the group must travel from one bank of the river to the other by stepping only on the resources (spot markers) they have been given. If a group member "falls into the river," the group starts over. Also, if one of the resources isn't being stood on, stepped on, or touched by a group member, even momentarily, they might lose it to the river (the facilitator confiscates it to represent this misfortune). The message we are sending is that we need to value our recovery tools.

Processing Points: Was it difficult for the group to maintain a sense of connection with each other during this activity? Generally, as people become physically distant from each other, it becomes more difficult to maintain a sense of connectedness. Did this happen during the activity? What kind of support were group members able to offer and take from one another? In what ways did this feel similar to or different from the ways in which they support each other more generally?

Cup Pyramid

Materials Needed: 21 or more large plastic cups
Approximate Time: 15 minutes
Description: Start with a stack of 21 large plastic drinking cups, available at most grocery stores. Each group member removes a cup from the stack and

places it, mouth down, on a table or floor so that six cups are in a line. Group members then continue to remove cups from the stack, one at a time, but the next five cups get placed on top of the first row of six cups, pyramid style. This process continues until a six-level cup pyramid has been built, with a single cup on the top level. To increase the challenge, you can use a seven-cup base for a seven-level cup pyramid, or a 15-cup base to go up even higher. Once the pyramid has been built, the next task is for the group to dismantle it in reverse fashion with each person removing one cup at a time and restacking it on the pile. The group should be able to construct and dismantle the pyramid without any cups falling in the process. Time the group, and then challenge them to improve upon their time.

Processing Points: How did the group work together to accomplish the task? Were they able to get out of each other's way during the process? What factors contributed to the improved time? Where else in life can we improve our outcomes though a similar process?

Source: Cavert and Thompson, 2017.

Ball, Cup, Bandana Flip

Materials Needed: A bandana, a plastic cup, and a ping pong or tennis ball for every four people in your group

Approximate Time: 10 minutes

Description: Adopting a new behavior can be challenging, whether it is following a new diet, starting an exercise routine, or learning a new language. This challenge helps to instill an appreciation for the process of practicing a new behavior.

Ask each group of four to start by holding the corner of a bandana so that it is taut and can support an upside-down plastic cup with a ball resting on top (actually this is the bottom of an upside-down cup). Explain that the challenge is to get the ball into the cup without touching either the ball or the cup. Only the corners of the bandana can be manipulated to make the cup flip occur. This alone will take most groups a few minutes to practice before they become somewhat comfortable with the process. After each group has been successful, explain that they have five minutes to complete as many flips as they can.

Processing Points: Much has been written about habit formation. Charles Duhigg (2012) and others have emphasized the importance of habit development. What feelings came up in your group members as they struggled to learn a new routine? Why do we tend to be so impatient with ourselves when trying to learn a new skill, and how can we increase our patience with ourselves and others as we strive to develop new ways of living? The aphorism "Anything worth doing is worth doing poorly at first" may apply.

Source: Cavert and Thompson, 2017.

Chapter Fourteen

No Prop Day

Pure Fun — Willingness Not Included

All group leaders have had the experience of running short on preparation time. This sequence will come in handy in such situations, or if and when you find yourself called upon for an impromptu program. Hammond and Cavert (2003) and others (Rhonke & Grout, 1998) have written whole books about activities that require nothing more than an open playing area and a group of willing participants. The No Prop activities included here are among my favorites, and they tend to work well with therapeutic populations. Please note that there are several other No Prop activities described for Word Day (chapter 8), Numbers Day (chapter 10), and other chapters of this book, so please feel free to integrate these into your No Prop Day sequence.

QUESTION OF THE DAY

What is something you enjoy doing that requires nothing more than yourself? Various forms of exercise (walking, running, calisthenics, etc.) come to mind, as well as meditation and daydreaming (a pastime that may be giving way to technology). Most people would not be willing to mention masturbation, though the question could stimulate (if you'll excuse the phrase) the idea of talking about something potentially shameful in a group, which might be in and of itself therapeutic. Know your audience, and please feel free to start with a different question.

After the go-round, you can comment that the repertoire of what is possible when no outside materials are required becomes infinitely greater when collaborating with others. Explain that you have a sequence of activities you would like to share with the group and all that is required is their willingness.

NO PROP DAY ACTIVITIES

Rain

Materials Needed: None
Approximate Time: 5–10 minutes
Description: With your group members seated in a circle, explain that you are going to "make rain" using only your hands. The more people involved the better, but the effect can be obtained with as few as 10. First, teach your group members several ways of making rain-like sounds, beginning with rubbing both open palms together to signify a misty drizzle. This is followed by collective finger-snapping that creates a sense of light rain. Next comes gentle but rapid tapping of one's thighs with both hands, suggesting an increase in the storm's intensity, and finally, open-hand clapping, evoking a real downpour.

Say that you will be leading the group in creating an ever-changing weather pattern. Their job is to follow your lead, by listening to and watching you. Take the group through a couple of rounds of all three stages, and pause. Now explain that next time the group will begin together, but anyone can make the decision to transform the sound. The idea is for everyone to listen attentively and be willing to play along. Continue for enough time so that several people in the group get an opportunity to lead the group in changing the sound.

Processing Points: What came up for people during this activity? Was anyone reminded of an experience during which they were caught in a heavy rain or maybe even enjoyed being outdoors in the rain? How did group members decide to take the initiative to lead or not, and how does this decision-making process generally work for them?

> I led this activity with an adolescent group, and one participant said that the sound of rain made her think about tears. This led to other group members talking about very painful memories, ones that had brought tears. One girl talked about her parents' decision to divorce and another talked about having lost a friend to a drug overdose. This then led to a brief psycho-educational session about drug abuse. In sum, a very emotional processing session had spontaneously arisen out of an ice-breaker. This is an example of a spontaneous metaphor inspiring people to share their thoughts, feelings, and experiences with each other. In other words, in this instance ABC indirectly led the group to discuss important topics that otherwise may have gone unexplored.

"Wah"

Materials Needed: None

Approximate Time: 5–10 minutes

Description: Ask your group members to stand in a circle about an arm's length distance from the people to their immediate right and left. Explain that just one word is required to play this game: "Wah." Ask your group members to repeat the word: "Wah." Next, explain that there is a sequence of gestures that are designed to accompany the word. Demonstrate for the group moving both hands above your head into prayer position, and say, "Wah" while your hands are over your head. Ask everyone in the group to repeat that sound and motion. Then explain that after a person raises their arms and says, "Wah," those to their immediate right and left raise their arm that is closest to the person in the middle who now has both arms raised (we'll call that person the middle person)—see the top figure on the next page. The middle person chooses the next middle person by making eye contact with someone else in the circle and saying "Wah" while bringing his or her hands down to chest level (see the bottom figure on the next page), indicating that it is now that person's turn to begin the sequence anew. The pair on either side of the current middle person (we'll call them the wing people) complete the sequence before the new one begins by bringing their arms down and saying, yes, you guessed it, "Wah!" Immediately after that, whoever has been indicated as the next middle person starts the sequence again by raising his or her hands overhead and saying, "Wah," and so on and so forth.

To clarify, the sequence goes as follows:

Middle person: Raises arms overhead in prayer position and says, "Wah."

Wing people: Each raises the arm that is closest to the middle person and says, "Wah."

Middle person: Makes eye contact with another group member, brings hands down to chest level to indicate the next middle person and says, "Wah."

Wing people: Complete the cycle by bringing their arms back down and saying, "Wah."

New middle person: Starts cycle from the beginning.

This game never fails to elicit giggles. It may take a minute or two for the group to fully master the directions, but once they do, they can really begin to play together. It effortlessly engages people, physically and emotionally.

Processing Points: What was the most difficult aspect of this activity? For some people, it might be learning the sequence of gestures; for others, it might be making eye contact with fellow group members; and for others still, it might be simply allowing themselves to be spontaneous. Do these dynamics hold true elsewhere? You can also discuss what about it was enjoyable

"Wah." *Photo by Ben Silverman.*

"Wah." *Photo by Ben Silverman*

.

(laughing together, being silly, trying something new, etc.). Are there other areas of their lives where they would like to experience these qualities? If so, which ones, and what would it take to enliven other situations in their lives?

Nonverbal Lineups

Materials Needed: None

Approximate Time: 10–15 minutes

Description: Explain that the next sequence of activities will be done without speaking. You might want to emphasize this as most people are accustomed to relying heavily on speech to communicate their ideas, wishes, and needs. I have rarely seen a group remain silent throughout this activity, even when I have been specific with the directive.

Say that you would like the group members to arrange themselves in order, *without talking*, according to specific criteria that you will mention. Start with having the group line up alphabetically according to their first names. The difficulty of this will depend largely on how long the group has been working together. After the group seems to have reached a consensus, check the results by asking each person to state their name. If errors were made, ask the group members to rearrange themselves accordingly, and check the results again.

You might want to take a minute here to discuss why it was so challenging for group members to remain silent throughout the activity. Ask them to pay heightened attention to completing the next round without talking. Next, ask your group members to arrange themselves in order of birth dates, including months and days, but not years. People will tend to rely on hand gestures and finger counting to accomplish this. Again, after a consensus is reached that the group has completed its work, check their results by asking each person to announce the month and date (but not the year) of their birth. (If that day happens to be a group member's birthday, you might pause for musical interlude at this point.) Discuss ways in which people adapted to the "no talking" restriction, and then progress to the next round, if appropriate.

Explain that the previous two rounds were based on objective criteria, so there was a correct solution each time. Say that the next criterion will be of a subjective nature. Ask your group members to line up according to their influence in the group, from least influential at one end to most influential at the other, again doing this without talking. Obviously, this criterion will invite a collective moment of contemplation that is sure to be multifaceted. First, group members are likely to reflect on their own and others' influence in the group, and very quickly the question "Whose feelings will get hurt if we go through with this?" might enter their minds. Your group members might object to going through with the exercise based on the fact that it could be injurious to some members of the group. This in itself will make for a productive processing session.

Processing Points: The last round of this exercise is certainly the most emotionally challenging. Whether or not the group members decided to attempt to order themselves or not, you can discuss the characteristics that make for an influential group member (confidence, generating useful ideas, being helpful to others, etc.) and the opposite (silent, disinterested, tentative, etc.). You can also discuss the process of how the group went about organizing itself. Since the nature of the criterion was subjective, there was no right answer, so the process of addressing the question might itself become useful to explore. Of course, there are some concrete reasons why a person may be less influential than others—for example, being newer to the group.

Take a Stand

Materials Needed: None

Approximate Time: Varies, depending upon the number of criteria used and the extent of discussion following each round and following the activity as a whole

Description: This classic group process comes from a tradition of sociometry, and it can be used with large or small groups. Sociometry is a method of non-verbal self-disclosure whereby individuals reveal information about themselves by standing in a particular position along a continuum. It is often used in psychodrama groups (Dayton, 2005), as well as in experiential education settings. Take a Stand functions as an invitation to self-reflect and self-disclose, two important components of group counseling. The basic premise is that the room—or playing area if you are outdoors—is delineated as a continuum, and group members are invited to position themselves at either end of the spectrum or anywhere in between, according to the criteria you state. It is helpful to establish a marker of some kind at each end of the playing area—for example, "the end of the room with the door, and the end of the room with the clock." The categories move from superficial during the first few rounds to more personal as the sequence progresses. Please feel free to choose from the list that follows, or make up your own.

Do you prefer hot weather or cold weather?
Are you a night owl or a morning person?
Are you head-centered or heart-centered?
Do you believe in nature or nurture?
Are you an introvert or an extrovert?
Are you a dog person or a cat person?
Are you trusting or mistrustful?
Are you grateful or discontent?
Are you resentful or free of resentment?

Are you angry or joyous?

Are you self-involved or interested in others?

Do you believe in a higher power or not?

Are you a tortoise or a hare?

Are you tolerant or intolerant of those different from you?

Are you generous or stingy?

Are you serene or agitated?

Are you assertive or submissive?

Are you kind or mean-spirited and vengeful?

Are you willing to admit faults or self-righteous?

Are you truthful or do you put on airs?

Are you humble or arrogant?

Are you consistent or erratic?

Are you judgmental or accepting of others?

Are you accepting or critical of yourself?

Processing Points: You can progress rapidly from one category to the next, or you can pause between rounds to discuss why people placed themselves where they did. In some instances, it can be helpful to expand on how you define the various criteria (see the description of Take a Stand in chapter 18). Obviously, the categories later in the sequence lead to richer conversations than those nearer the beginning. Was it easier for group members to self-disclose knowing that everyone else was also making themselves vulnerable? How does this dynamic hold true in other settings? Were your group members surprised to find that they had things in common with other group members? Did they learn anything new about themselves or others?

Categories

Materials Needed: None

Approximate Time: 10 minutes

Description: Like Take a Stand (above), this activity offers your group members an opportunity to identify subgroups within the group as a whole, but now you will use the four corners of the room rather than a continuum. This activity can be a useful way of breaking up cliques in your group, if they exist, as it creates new subgroups. The following are some examples of categories you might consider using. Be sure to select some sets that will work well with your group.

Favorite Movie Genre (drama, fantasy, science fiction, comedy, or documentary)

Favorite Reading Material (periodicals [including magazines or newspapers], fiction, nonfiction, or electronic media)

Favorite Vacation Spot (the beach, the mountains, cities, or the country-
side)

Birth Order in Family of Origin (oldest, middle, youngest, or singleton)

After each round allow a few minutes for the subgroups to chat about what
drew them to this particular designation. In the case of favorites, you can
allow time for each person to share a specific trip, movie, book, etc. with his
or her subgroup. After the birth-order division, you can give a thumbnail
synopsis of birth-order theory and explain that each position has its advantages and its challenges. For example, oldest children tend to develop an
aptitude for leadership, but they often take on more responsibility than is
good for them; middles tend to get along well with a wide range of people
but they can get lost in the mix, and youngest siblings tend to get a lot of
attention for being "cute," and they are often good-natured and like to have
fun, but they may feel challenged in assuming positions of authority. Only
children tend to be accommodating and easy to get along with, much like
middles, but they may lack a competitive side. Ask your group members
whether the stated qualities or experiences ring true for them.

After offering several objective categories such as those described above,
explain that the next criteria will be abstract. You are going to invite group
members to identify with an inanimate object. Ask your group members to
imagine a canoe being paddled down a river. Do they identify with the canoe,
the paddle, the banks of the river, or the water? Assign a corner of the room
to each of these inanimate things and ask your group members to move to
one of these areas according to what they most closely identify with. Allow
time for the members of each small group to discuss what drew them to that
group, and then ask a member from each small group to share with the larger
group what came out of the discussion. Another more abstract set of categories might be parts of a car: do people identify with the exterior, the engine,
the dashboard and controls, or the interior seating?

Processing Points: Were you surprised to find you had certain things in
common with specific members of the group? Did you find yourself grouped
with the same person or people throughout the sequence? What else occurred
to you during the activity?

Jump for Joy

Materials Needed: None

Approximate Time: About three minutes per participant

Description: Jump for Joy is essentially a supported jump. The notion of
support is ubiquitous in group therapy. The supported jump is an intervention
that was developed by Ron Kurtz and used by Pat Ogden and Bonnie Goldstein at the Sensorimotor Psychotherapy Institute to help patients get in touch
with a feeling of joyfulness. The process of using one's own initiative to

become physically elevated is amplified by the group's support. The person jumping gets to set the pace and timing of the jump. Other group members boost the jumper by pushing up on the jumper's upper arms and elbows on the jumper's count of "One, two, three!" The jumper jumps on their own "three!" while the other group members lift him or her into the air.

Take time to negotiate the tactile contact involved with this activity. Especially in mixed gender groups, it will be important to negotiate a sense of safety. Limiting the boosters' contact to the arms and upper body of the jumper may help to minimize the possibility of boundary violations that could be experienced with support of the lower body. However, larger individuals might benefit from the additional support provided by lower-body support. Again, discussing the process prior to enacting it is advisable.

Processing Points: It's important to take time after the jump to allow the participants to process the experience and talk about what it felt like to receive that much support. Pat Ogden and Bonnie Goldstein (2018) suggest that Jump for Joy can provide a temporary respite from the visceral feeling of hopelessness that many patients experience. Ask your group members to reflect on where else in their lives they would like to experience more joy

Jump for Joy. *Photo by the author.*

and hopefulness. By providing a physical representation of these qualities, Jump for Joy conveys that such change is possible.

Source: Pat Ogden and Bonnie Goldstein, keynote address at the 2018 AGAP annual meeting.

Point-Yes

Materials Needed: None

Approximate Time: 5 minutes

Description: This deceptively simple game can spark some important conversations about consent. The premise is simple enough: with the group members standing in a circle, one member of the group makes eye contact with another group member and points at that person and then waits for a non-verbal indication of yes or no. If a no is given, the person pointing keeps pointing and making eye contact with different group members until they receive an affirmative response. Upon receiving a yes, the pointer moves to take the permission-giver's place, but not until that person has gained permission to take yet another person's place. Feel free to play several rounds, and for groups larger than 15 or 16, you might want to have two games in play at once so as to keep everyone engaged.

Processing Points: What are some instances in which action was taken without your consent? Are there instances in which you wish that your opinion had been taken into consideration before action was taken? How do we know when we have gained another person's consent, and when is it especially important to get it before taking action? The issue of sexual consent is experiencing a watershed moment in the United States, with the Me Too movement inspiring many people to come forward with stories about how they were sexually approached or engaged with without having given their consent. This activity can open the door for these kinds of conversations.

Depending on where your group members want to go with these questions, issues concerning disloyalty, deception, and even boundary violations can come up. Even if they are not overtly spoken about, asking questions concerning consent is likely to get your group members thinking about some difficult issues.

Look Up-Look Down

Materials Needed: None

Approximate Time: 5 minutes

Description: This activity builds on the eye contact established during Point-Yes, described above. The group members begin by standing in a circle; the therapist explains that he or she will say, "Look down" and "Look up" alternately. The group members are asked to follow these simple directions. As group members look up, they should pick one person in the group with whom to try to establish eye contact. Those whose gazes are met with another's upon looking up step out of circle while those who do not are asked to remain in the circle. You can play a few rounds and then stop to discuss before starting over. This game is paradoxical in that those who fail to make eye contact with others get to play the longest. In most situations, we get to "play longer" through establishing and maintaining a connection with others.

Processing Points: What does it mean to be available to others? What feelings came up for people when they either made contact with someone else or were left out? What factors contribute to whether or not we stay connected to other people? What factors keep us isolated? Bear in mind that these questions, and the activity, can be painful for those who have trouble establishing and maintaining relationships with others. Feeling left out of a group can be a painful experience, and this activity can bring those feelings up. If your group members are willing, you can discuss other times when they have felt left out or unable to form a meaningful connection with others.

Source: Chris Cavert at a TEAM conference.

Galloping Hands

Materials Needed: None
Approximate Time: 10 minutes
Description: This one works especially well with groups that are larger than 12 but can be done effectively with as few as eight or nine. This activity is done from a seated position, either in chairs or sitting cross-legged on the floor. Ask your group members if any of them play an instrument, and if so, you can digress for a brief inquiry into their musical lives. Next explain that you are going to teach everyone how to play a percussive instrument. They will accomplish this by cupping their hand and bringing it down on their thigh. It should make a "thud" sound when done properly. Give your group members an opportunity to practice this a few times.

The first challenge will be for the "thuds" to move around the circle in order, from left to right. Watch carefully to see that the correct pattern is maintained, and after it has been, encourage your group to try going a bit faster. Then you can reverse directions and try going the other way with the same guidelines. Again, after the pattern has been mastered, try going faster.

Here's where the real fun begins. Remind people that they have the right to say no (building on the skills they worked on during Point-Yes) if they are uncomfortable with what you will be asking them to do. Then explain that everyone should put their right hand on the thigh of the person to their immediate right, and place their left hand on the thigh of the person to their immediate left. Explain that the guidelines remain as in the prior two rounds, that is, the "thuds" should progress around the circle in order, in whatever direction is chosen. If a mishap occurs, you will ask the group to begin again. The challenge is for the group to complete a successful cycle around the circle with no mistakes. This activity can require patience and it pushes most people to the edge of their comfort zone due to the physical contact involved, so proceed accordingly.

Processing Points: How uncomfortable did this activity make your group members and why? I suggest that you make issues related to touch speakable. Touch is most often reserved for handshakes, violence, and sexual situations, but when else might touch be appropriate? You might consider discussing various gestures of encouragement in sports such as pats on the back and hugs.

Source: Karl Rhonke at a TEAM conference.

Chapter Fifteen

Animal Day

Let Your Essence Shine

Animals are an important part of our world. In many cases, people who have experienced very difficult or traumatic relationships with their fellow humans find the relationships they develop with four-legged creatures to be happier. Animal-assisted therapy has become increasingly popular, and many people take comfort in the unconditional love of a pet dog or snuggly cat. Even memories of a treasured pet can create tender feelings. Most animals, except for human beings, do not lose their ability to play as they age, and some very enjoyable activities have been inspired by or named for various furry creatures. I present a few of them in this chapter.

QUESTION OF THE DAY

What is your favorite pet you have ever had and what was or is special about it? Or what animal do you most identify with? What qualities of a particular animal speak to you? For example, one person might relate to the curiosity of a monkey, another to the energy of a leopard, and so on.

ANIMAL DAY ACTIVITIES

Speed Rabbit

> **Materials Needed:** None
> **Approximate Time:** 10 minutes

Rabbit. *Photo by Ben Silverman.*

Elephant. *Photo by Ben Silverman.*

Sailboat. *Photo by Ben Silverman*.

Description: This ice-breaker provides an opportunity for your group members to play spontaneously and practice looking silly in front of each other. If they can tolerate the embarrassment associated with this game, perhaps they can better tolerate the painful material they will be working on in other components of their treatment.

With the group members standing in a circle, ask for two volunteers to come into the middle and stand in a row with you, shoulder to shoulder. Explain that you are going to create various moving figures by coordinating your efforts. Start with a rabbit by having each person on the outside stomp their outer leg while the person in the middle makes bunny ears above his or her head by making peace signs with both hands. Ask the other group members to practice making rabbits too, in groups of three.

Ask for two more volunteers to demonstrate making an elephant with you. I usually maintain the middle position during these demonstrations. For the elephant, the outer two people make elephant ears by leaning outward and using their arms to form gigantic ears while the middle person uses his or her arms to create the trunk. Ask the other group members to form groups of three and practice making elephants in a similar fashion.

Ask for two new volunteers to help you demonstrate Jell-O. This is done by the outer pair forming a bowl around the person in the middle. The middle person jiggles as if he or she were made out of gelatin. This never fails to elicit some chuckles from the group. Finally, ask for the last pair of volunteers to help you demonstrate a sailboat, with the outside pair creating the hull of the boat as the middle person forms the sail. Ask others to practice in groups of three after each demonstration. Also, feel free to create your own three-person creations (a toaster, perhaps?).

Explain that practicing making the moving sculptures was all preparation for a game called Speed Rabbit. One person stands in the middle of the circle and points to somebody, calling out the name of one of the creations that were just practiced (Rabbit, Elephant, Jell-O, or Sailboat). The challenge is for whomever is pointed at to create the moving statue along with the people to his or her immediate right and left before the person in the middle can say, "Zippity-zappity-zoo." If any one of the three people fails to join in with the correct action during the allotted time, they become the next person in the middle of the circle. A group member can also find their way into the center by joining a sculpture without being one of the designated three players. Be sure to allow plenty of time for the practice rounds before you start in earnest. If some of your group members have trouble uttering "Zippity-zappity-zoo" quickly, it could take them a long time to get out of the middle. Allow enough time for several people to have turns in the middle.

Processing Points: What was difficult about this activity, if anything? Was being spontaneous challenging? What about looking foolish in front of other group members? When else do people worry about how they appear to others? What value do you see in this? The great CBT psychologist Albert Ellis was a proponent of what he called "shame-attacking exercises" (1996). In other words, doing something in spite of the shame it triggers is a good way to become inured to toxic shame. Participating in Speed Rabbit may be useful along these lines.

Bees in a Hive

Materials Needed: A 40-foot length of rope that can be tied into a large circle, and a soft ball that will not hurt people if they get hit with it, such as a foam ball or soft playground ball

Approximate Time: 10 minutes

Description: Divide your group into two approximately equal groups. This process can itself become a mini-activity if you use a creative means of dividing the group. I suggest using a few of the categories listed in Take a Stand (chapter 14) until you get a more-or-less even split—a difference of one or two between the two groups is fine. Alternatively, you can ask everyone whose name begins with "*A* through *L*" to stand on one side and everyone whose name begins with "*M* through *Z*" to stand on the other. If it's a newer group, ask people to say their name aloud after they have divided into two groups.

Make the large rope into a circle and place it on the ground. Ask one group to go into the middle of the circle and the other group to stand outside the circle. Explain that those inside the circle are the "Bees" and those on the outside are the "Beekeepers." Think of this game like circular dodgeball. The Beekeepers start with a light, squishy ball that they will throw at the Bees. If a Bee is hit, they become a Beekeeper and they move into the Beekeeper group with the ball. The Beekeepers may pass the ball among themselves before throwing it at a Bee. If, however, the ball is caught by one of the Bees, the person who threw the ball moves into the center and becomes a Bee. Play a round until all the group members are either Bees or Beekeepers or until there are just a few people left in one of the groups. Play another round with people who started as Bees the first time starting as Beekeepers this time and vice versa. Caution your group members to avoid throwing the ball at each other's heads.

Processing Points: What feelings came up in group members as their subgroup grew or shrank in number and they gradually became part of a majority or minority group? Do we feel more empowered when we are part of a majority? Can your group members share experiences of having been part of a majority or minority group? What are the associated thoughts and feelings? In addition to talking generally about these categories within society, you can explore how these variables can be circumstantial. For example, a Jewish or Muslim individual living in the United States may feel as though they are part of a minority group most of the time except when they attend religious services or visit a store or neighborhood that sells foods intended to support their faith. Did group members feel concerned that they might disappear altogether as their group's numbers shrank? Building on the faith-based example above, this could relate to intermarriage as fewer and fewer people identify solidly with a specific religion.

You can also use this activity to discuss risk-taking. The risk of throwing the ball is that it might get caught, but the price of not throwing it is stagnation. Where else in life does avoidance of risk constitute procrastination? Not asking someone on a date or not applying for a job or requesting a change in work schedule are some examples of this dynamic. Can you think of others?

Fish/Fly/Bear Puzzle

Materials Needed: One chair for each group member plus one empty chair. Additional props are optional for this activity. I sometimes use old CDs to identify flies and small rubber discs to identify fish, but you can work with your groups to have them impersonate the three creatures in their own ways. It's important that all members of the group can distinguish who is playing which part.

Approximate Time: 10 minutes

Description: With your group members seated in a circle with one extra chair, divide them evenly into "Fish," "Flies," and "Bears" by asking them to count off that way ("Fish-Fly-Bear-Fish-Fly-Bear . . ."). It is useful to use a prop to identify two of the three groups. For example, you can use floppy rubber discs to designate fish and old CDs to designate flies since the discs themselves will fly if tossed properly. Ask every third group member to hold one of the objects or otherwise make themselves into a Fish, Fly, or Bear. To increase the challenge, forgo the props, and use pantomime, as in the Speed Rabbit activity. The Bears can put their hands over their heads to appear large. The Flies can form wings, and the Fish can form "fish mouths" though this might be hard to maintain throughout the game.

Make sure there is one unoccupied chair in the circle. Explain that the challenge for the group is to end up so that all like-creatures are seated together. However, they can only move according to the rules of nature. Bears like to eat fish, so Bears can cross over Fish to occupy an empty seat. Fish like to eat flies, so Fish can pass Flies to move into the open seat, and flies like to nibble on bears, so Flies can pass Bears to take an open seat. These rules may be confusing at first, but should become clear with a demonstration.

Most groups experience a learning curve with this one. Once they get the hang of it, it starts to move along. Usually one or two group members will start directing the others, so you might want to note this and integrate it into your discussion afterward.

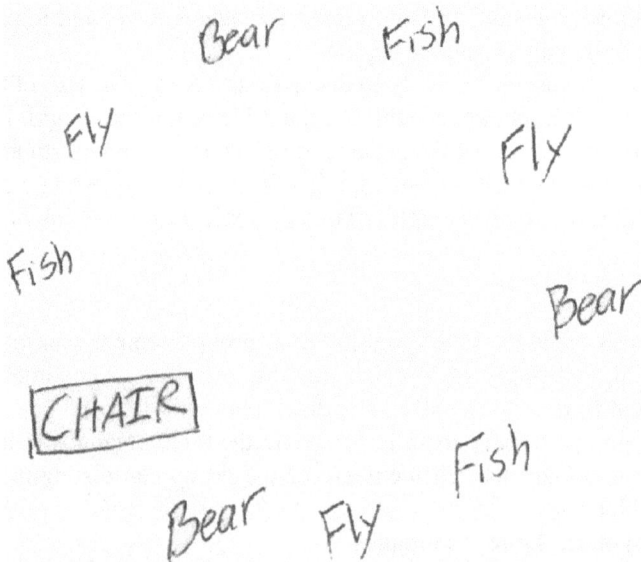

Fish/Fly/Bear Puzzle setup. *Photo by the author.*

Processing Points: What was it like to learn something new? Does this remind you of some aspect of your recovery or treatment? What role did you find yourself in during the activity? Was it a familiar role? If you took on a lot of responsibility for solving the puzzle, was this because you wanted to get recognized in some way? Was it important for you to be in control? Where else does this occur?

Source: Sikes, 1998.

Mouse Traps

Materials Needed: A supply of wooden mouse traps, available at hardware stores, some of which have been "dummied" by you beforehand; some blindfolds; and a way to define two ends of a playing area (you can use tape, rope, or furniture for this purpose). You can "dummy" some of the mousetraps by using pair of needle-nose pliers and twisting the small piece of metal that extends through the catch that would normally be triggered by a mouse. Once you accomplish this, the trap is effectively inoperable, but it creates the illusion of a set trap! The main advantage of using dummied traps along with some live ones is that it saves time during set up of the activity. The dummied traps also create the illusion of real danger while minimizing the actual risk.

Approximate Time: 20–30 minutes

Description: Activities involving mousetraps have been written about elsewhere (Sikes, 2003). They're very effective tools for helping people expand their sense of trust and positive risk-taking. I present two of my favorites here. The first activity involves giving everyone a mousetrap and teaching them how to set and release the trap without getting hurt (make sure that you practice sufficiently on your own before trying to teach others these skills). The key to safe handling of a mousetrap is holding it by its edges and not putting one's fingers near the top of the trap.

Traps that have been set should be placed gently down on the floor or a table, *making sure to hold only the sides of the trap.* To release a trap, a light tap with the sole of a shoe works fine, or for those who would like to try something a bit more adventurous, a trap can be safely set off by placing a palm slowly and firmly down on top of the trap. This pressure will release the lock. The bar will not snap back until the hand is quickly lifted off the trap. You can demonstrate this for your group members, reminding them that many of the activities you present are based on perceived, as opposed to actual, risk. In truth, there is some minimal real risk associated with playing with mouse traps. Releasing them by hand, as described above, can result in some mild sensation. Stepping on a live mouse trap while wearing shoes is unlikely to cause pain, though doing so while wearing just socks, for example, may result in a bit of a stinging sensation but no injury beyond that.

Accepting guidance to avoid painful situations. *Photo by Ben Silverman.*

Allow anyone who wants to try setting off a trap by hand to do so. Allow those who do not to go at their own pace. Some will have enough vicarious anxiety by simply watching others play with the traps.

For the second activity, ask each person to set a trap and place it in the middle of an open space you have prepared. The open space should ideally be at least 20 feet long and a boundary should be defined by a marker at either end. This can be a piece of rope, a strip of tape, or some furniture off to the side. Traps should be approximately two to three feet apart and in a random pattern within the space. Add 10 or more additional traps that look as if they are live but which you have actually made into "dummy" traps beforehand. Be sure to place the dummy traps down gently to create the illusion that they are live.

Explain that you are offering your group members an opportunity to increase their trust in each other by walking blindfolded through the maze of mousetraps. Group members should choose a partner with whom they would like to develop greater trust and enhanced communication. The sighted person in each pair offers verbal direction to his or her partner from outside the perimeter so that the partner passes safely through the "minefield." Some people might need physical support to navigate the minefield. If so, you may allow the guide into the minefield to offer a helping hand. After all pairs have had a turn, take a moment to talk as a group about what was helpful to the blindfolded people as they navigated the maze. Then the blindfolds are given to the other partner in each pair, and they in turn are led through the maze by their partner. Alternatively, you can have each participant select their own guide after they have guided someone.

The level of challenge of this activity can be adjusted by footwear worn or not worn as well as the distance between the traps. Offer your group members the option of keeping their shoes on throughout, waking in just socks, or going barefoot. Depending on the width of your playing area, you can probably have two pairs working simultaneously.

Processing Points: This activity is rich with metaphorical application. What "traps" do your group members need to avoid in their lives? What situations can cause problems if they stumble into them without adequate protection? Conversely, what safeguards do your group members put in place to help them avoid such pitfalls? For people in recovery from addiction, this might include calling one's sponsor regularly and working the 12 Steps. The guide in this activity functions much as a 12 Step sponsor does, staying closely connected to his or her charge and helping them remain on the path to improved health. This activity is sure to spark a meaningful discussion about how people develop and maintain trusting relationships.

Source: Sikes, 2003.

Chapter Sixteen

Balloon Day

Finding the Levity within You

Balloons are unique in their ability to conjure up memories of childhood. They are associated with birthday parties, carnival games, the circus, water balloon fights, and so on. The lazy pace with which they drift through the air provides an antidote to our hectic lives. Put a balloon in the air, and people, no matter their age, will want to play with it. Think of the random balloon that gets batted around the audience at a concert or sporting event. When else in life will adults spontaneously start playing with each other?

The activities presented here all use balloons as the primary prop. In addition to emphatically saying, "Play with me," balloons are much less partial to the athletically gifted than are their rounded counterparts (baseballs, for example). Their slow and often random flight patterns are inviting to people of all ages and abilities. It is also nearly impossible to get injured by a balloon. Depending on which activities you choose, you might want to begin your session by asking for help inflating the balloons. This functions as a subversive deep-breathing exercise.

QUESTION OF THE DAY

What associations do you have with balloons, and can you recall a specific balloon memory you would like to share with the group?

BALLOON DAY ACTIVITIES

Tap

Materials Needed: One inflated balloon per group member and a stopwatch

Approximate Time: 10 minutes

Description: This is similar to Moon Ball, described in chapter 7, except balloons are used instead of a beach ball. Begin by launching a balloon in the air and see if the group can keep it suspended in the air for 30 seconds, according to the following guideline: Each person can touch the balloon just once before someone else touches it. Now, following the same rules, introduce a second balloon, and repeat. Keep adding balloons until there is one balloon in the air per group member. The challenge is for the group to keep *all* the balloons suspended for the specified period of time, up to one minute.

Processing Points: At what point did the activity become unmanageable? Was there a point at which it was optimally fun (not so easy that it was boring but not so difficult that it became impossible)? When else in life would you like to function in the "optimally fun" or optimally challenging zone? When have you been bored and when have you felt overwhelmed? How did you respond to these situations?

Also, did the group find an effective way to adapt to the increasing demands of the added balloons? How did this happen? Did specific group members play key roles? Was everyone involved?

Balloon Volleyball

Materials Needed: A supply of inflated balloons, boundary markers, and a net or net equivalent

Approximate Time: 15 minutes

Description: This self-explanatory activity builds on the skills developed in Tap, described above. This version of volleyball can be played seated (great for seniors) or standing. You need to define a playing area and a "net." Depending upon the space, the whole room can be the playing area, with a table functioning as the net for a seated version of the game. For groups who prefer to stand, clear away any chairs and use a rope or other material to form a net that is about as tall as most of your group members. The rules of volleyball apply, except you are playing with a balloon. Serve one balloon at a time. Each team member may tap the balloon once before a teammate taps it, and each team is allowed a maximum of three taps and then the balloon must cross over the net. If a balloon happens to pop while in play, that is an indication that your group members have become engaged in the activity.

Bring in one of your spares, and keep your group playing until the momentum seems to have peaked.

Processing Points: Take a minute or two to reflect on the fun that your group members were having. Did they forget about thoughts that tend to bother them? What factors enabled them to play freely, and where else might they be able to find these ingredients?

Balloon Floor Hockey

Materials Needed: A few inflated balloons and a pool noodle for each group member. It is best if you have two sets of different colored noodles, one color for each team. Also, goals should be defined at either end of the playing area.

Approximate Time: 15 minutes

Description: All furniture should be cleared away as much as possible to maximize participants' ability to move freely around the space. Divide your group into two teams and explain that in Balloon Floor Hockey, the task is that each team tries to get the balloon into the opposing team's goal, just as in ice hockey, except balloons and pool noodles are used instead of pucks and hockey sticks. Also, there is less physical contact in Balloon Floor Hockey!

Explain that the balloon can only be touched by the pool noodles, not by anyone's hands. Allow the teams to deploy themselves in specific positions, if they care to. Balloons are highly breakable, so have a few extra inflated balloons on hand in case one pops. Caution your group members to only strike the balloon when it is at knee height or lower. This should minimize people accidentally hitting each other with the noodles.

Processing Points: This game invites the group to be playfully competitive with each other and offers a safe outlet for some aggression to emerge. The combination of the competitive nature of the game and the novel materials used allow the child within each of us to come out and play. Explore with your group members what feelings arose in them amid all the excitement of the game. Did the experience trigger memories of competing as part of a team? What were those former experiences like and how was this one similar or different?

Balloon Sculptures

Materials Needed: 100 or more inflated balloons, several rolls of Scotch tape, and some markers

Approximate Time: 30 minutes

Description: The first task is to inflate all those balloons! Depending upon the stamina of your group members, you can ask them to help you with

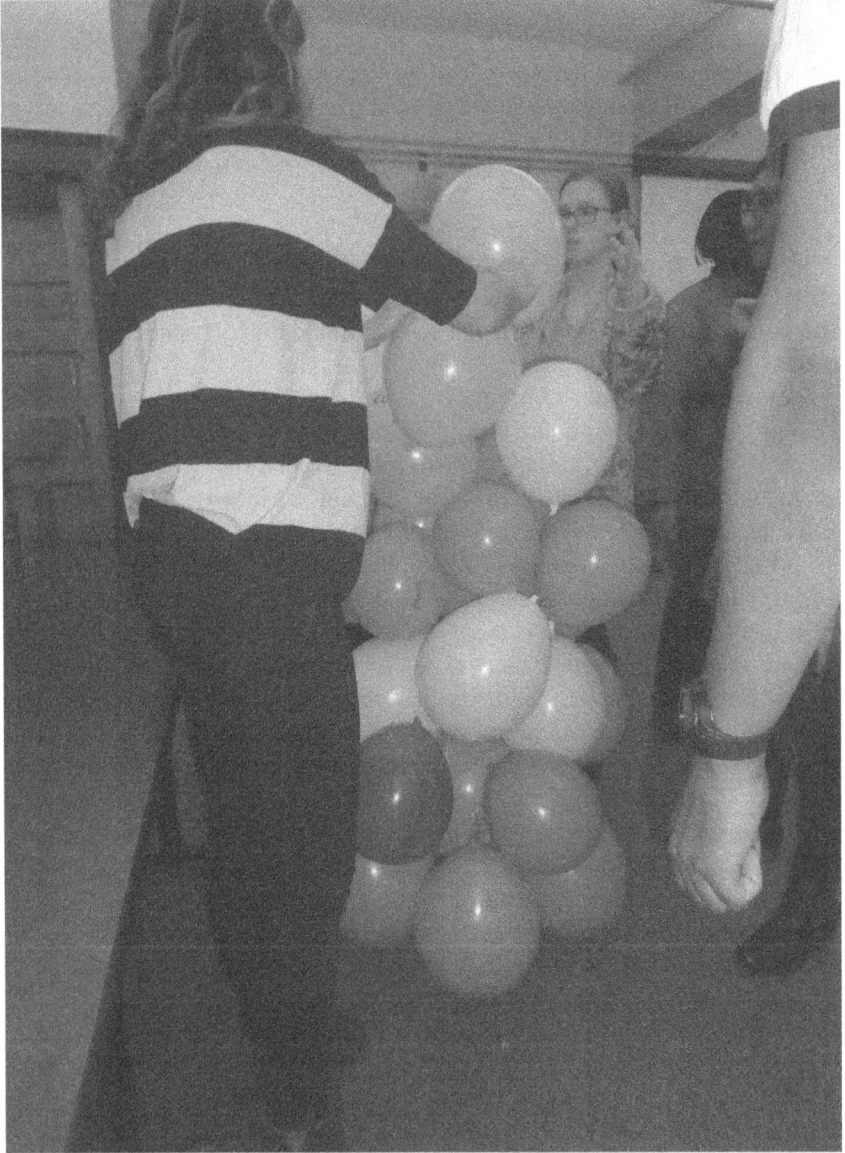

Creating art out of an inflated sense of our triggers. *Photo by the author.*

this. Otherwise, you might want to have a pump or provide pre-inflated balloons.

Explain that the group has an opportunity to transform their triggers into something beautiful during this activity. Ask your group members to use the markers to write their triggers on the balloons. Ask each group member to write one unique trigger on each of five or more balloons. Once most of the balloons have been designated "triggers," divide your group into smaller groups of three to five each. Divide the balloons so that each group has approximately the same number of balloons (at least 15–20 per small group). Give each small group a roll of clear tape and explain that they have 10 minutes to construct the tallest free-standing sculpture they can using only the balloons provided and the roll of tape you have given them. You might give a two-minute warning, and when time is up, you can measure the height of the various sculptures if you want to increase the competitive energy, or you can simply admire the creations that your group members have made. While the overall tone of ABC is cooperative, occasionally introducing some good-natured competition can increase groups members' enthusiasm and focus during the activity.

After the group has taken time to appreciate each other's sculptures, say that people will now have a chance to "pop," or destroy, their triggers. This can be done using pushpins or, more aggressively, by jumping on each balloon. The noise created by the mass popping can itself be triggering to some people, so give your group members an opportunity to leave the room during this time, if they wish.

Processing Points: How did it feel to pop all those balloons? Were your group members able to ventilate some anger during the popping? What are some other ways they might be able to diminish their triggers? Of course, in reality we can't simply pop our triggers and make them disappear. What methods have your group members used to effectively shrink and weaken their triggers? If we stick together, as we caused the balloons to do, we will be less susceptible to our triggers.

More importantly, how did the small groups collaborate during the construction of their sculptures? What relationships evolved within each small group and between the different groups? Did anyone consider pooling their resources with another small group so that both groups could contribute to making an even more impressive tower?

Source: David Flack at the 2014 AEE International Conference.

Part III

Adventure-Based Counseling for Recovery from Addiction

Chapter Seventeen

Walking the Walk

ABC and Recovery from Addiction

The metaphorical process of growth and change embedded in ABC can be useful to anyone engaged in a process of personal transformation, but it might be especially helpful to those who have turned to self-destructive behavior in a misguided quest for contact with other people. Charles Duhigg (2012) explains the "cue-routine-reward" cycle as central to habit formation, including addictive ones. He maintains that the key to behavioral change is finding a way to keep the cues and rewards constant but finding new ways of bridging them with new behaviors. It follows that adventure-based activities can be used to meet the social and psychological needs that some may have tried to meet though self-destructive behavior such as gambling, drug use, excessive internet surfing, and compulsive sexual activity. The operative cue in all these instances might be loneliness or boredom, and the reward after engaging in ABC becomes an enlivening experience accompanied by genuine human interaction, as opposed to the faux sense of connection that addictions offer.

A REVIEW OF THE LITERATURE

Addictions are a pervasive and growing epidemic in contemporary society. In addition to substance addictions such as alcohol, illicit drugs, and caffeine, process addictions, such as gambling, sex, and excessive internet use, work, and eating are also widespread (Korshak, Nickow, & Straus, 2014). Large-scale studies have not been done, but from reviewing the literature on addictions, Sussman, Lisha, and Griffiths (2011) estimate that at least 47% (146 million people) of the population of the United States suffer from the deleterious consequences of one or more addictive behaviors in any given year; 16% from substance addictions (including tobacco, alcohol, and illicit drugs but not caffeine, the most common addictive substance); and 31% from process addictions.

Process addictions are being increasingly recognized as an issue in the popular press, including notable work by Dokoupal (2012), who reports on widespread stress and mental disease related to misuse of technology, and Luscombe (2016), who writes about a modern syndrome known as porn-induced erectile disorder (PIED) in which young men who use pornography are no longer able to become aroused with a real partner. However, among the behavioral addictions, only Problem Gambling is recognized by the medical community as a legitimate diagnosis (American Psychiatric Association, 2013). Drug and alcohol abuse has received more widespread medical validation than the behavioral addictions, and treatment centers for substance abuse are abundant in the United States (though addicted populations are still largely underserved and often incarcerated or hospitalized without receiving treatment for their underlying addictions).

For most of the 20th century, approaches to treatment for alcoholism and other addictions fell short. Some clinicians who focused on the importance of abstinence were experienced as judgmental by their patients, while other clinicians, adhering to the theoretical orientation of their choice, ignored or minimized the addictive symptomatology (Freimuth, 2005). Either approach ended all too often in treatment failure. Advances in theoretical understanding in the last decade have given us the necessary principles for successful addiction treatment (Korshak & Delboy, 2013; Schwartz, Nickow, Arseneau, & Gisslow, 2015), and these include ample opportunities for mutual support. Roth (2004) adds that a key to successful recovery is becoming fully aware and accepting of oneself. Effective group psychotherapy provides both mutual support and opportunities for increased self-awareness. Currently, the favored forms of group treatment for addiction are CBT, 12 Step Facilitation, and Interpersonal Group Psychotherapy (Fletcher, 2013). Adjunctive, experientially oriented approaches such as Equine-Assisted Therapy (Kirby, 2016), Somatic Experiencing (Levine, 2010), and Yoga Therapy (Forbes, 2011) are all increasing in popularity. ABC is another emerging, innovative treatment modality that is particularly effective for this pandemic problem.

The elements of novelty and excitement that are central to ABC may be especially impactful for those who are plagued with addictions. Flores (2004) proposes that effective treatment for addiction requires (1) novelty, (2) arousal, and (3) support—all qualities that lie at the core of ABC. In his work with substance-abusing adolescents, Russell (2008) finds that many who successfully recovered through AT had previously failed at conventional treatment; something about the novelty of AT was unique in being able to impact these teenagers. I suspect that AT's uniqueness goes hand-in-hand with its ability to stimulate, a key to its success in treating addictions. Since addictions stimulate the mesocorticolimbic pathway, resulting in a powerful release of dopamine (the precursor for adrenaline), it follows that ABC, offering the natural stimulation that arises from the visceral experience of action, might be especially helpful for those recovering from addictions in that it can meet the needs that were previously met by self-destructive behavior (Korshak, Nickow, & Straus, 2014). Substitution is key to successful habit change. For example, ABC is especially appealing to recovering compulsive gamblers because destructive games of chance, such as casino gambling, are replaced by games and activities in which everybody wins, a basic tenet of ABC.

Flores (2004) characterizes the central problem of addiction as an attachment disorder. The operative cue in addictive activities, whether drug and alcohol use, gambling, or compulsive sexual activity, can be understood as loneliness. Just as AA often serves as a replacement for the sense of social connection and support that problem drinkers previously sought through drinking, ABC can function to help all recovering individuals feel connected to each other. In contrast to the faux connection that results from addictive behavior, leaving the user unsatisfied and merely wanting more, ABC creates a meaningful experience of genuine human connection and belonging. Per Duhigg's (2012) hypothesis, ABC is well-suited to alter the addictive cycle, offering a plethora of group activities that reward pro-social behavior while meeting the social and psychological needs of the individual.

There is a dearth of evidence-based research in the field of addictions as a whole, and less research on using ABC and other emerging treatment modalities (Sheff, 2013; Weiss et al., 2004). However, Gass and McPhee (1990) conducted a meta-analysis of addiction treatment programs that used AT as part of their treatment programming. Of the 61 programs surveyed, only two had conducted research to measure the effectiveness of the experiential interventions; in both cases, the research showed enhanced effectiveness of programs incorporating adventure. In one of the few evidence-based studies of ABC, Faulkner (2002) finds that problem-solving abilities improved in the participants after exposure to teams-course activities. He hypothesizes that problem-solving might be useful to patients involved in the recovery process because addiction is known to compromise problem-solving abilities. There is clearly a need for more research on using ABC as an effective treatment modality in recovery from addiction, but the widespread use of AT and ABC in addiction treatment programs suggests that research will continue to show enhanced effectiveness for such programs.

In spite of the lack of evidence-based studies, many theorists and practitioners have discussed the application of ABC in the literature of addiction treatment. Mackinnon (1998) and others (Quereau & Zimmermann, 1992;

Horne, 1997; Hagedorn & Hirshhorn, 2009) write about the theoretical application of ABC for addiction treatment. Gass and Dobkin (1988) and Gass (1995) offer sequences of activities designed to support recovery from addiction. Quereau and Zimmermann (1992) likewise describe an AT program designed to augment the process of recovery. Horne (1997) identifies an experiential activity to reflect each of AA's 12 steps. Gass, Gillis, and Russell (2012) provide several examples of using ABC activities for addiction treatment. O'Donnell (2014) captures the impressions of several addiction patients who participated in a high ropes course as part of their treatment, and she equates the fear that one patient felt as he jumped off the Power Pole (a jump from 30 feet up, relying only on the belay team below—see the last figure in chapter 2) to the fear he felt about living a sober life. I have previously written about an ABC program that captures many general principles of recovery, such as asking for help, and my program, described in detail in the following chapter, offers an activity for each of AA's 12 steps (Straus, 2013). Anecdotal reflections report effectiveness on multiple parameters such as a decrease in addictive engagement, enhanced socialization, and general gratification from recovery.

Other practitioners, theorists, and researchers have theorized that skills learned and practiced in ABC or AT might aid the recovery process. In their discussion of using ABC activities with recovering bulimics, Maguire and Priest (1994) posit that bulimics tend to be self-centered and therefore are likely to benefit from being team players. The same principle may apply to all recovering individuals; it is commonly thought that addiction leads to self-absorption and preoccupation with one thing: using. The collaboration required throughout ABC tacitly encourages participants to become aware of others, both inside and outside the treatment milieu.

THEORY INTO ACTION: ANECDOTES FROM THE FIELD

Itan (1998) notes that ABC sessions can generate stress and that when working with recovering populations, adventure therapists do well to directly address behaviors, thoughts, and feelings that relate closely to urges to use. These can be internally generated or brought on by stressful interactions that can occur during ABC programming. For example, anxiety can be generated when some group members want to give up on a challenge while others want to continue, or when two or more people have different approaches to the same problem-solving initiative. These situations offer opportunities for teaching "here and now" self-soothing and conflict-management techniques that can be used for navigating challenging situations outside the ABC group without resorting to drugs, alcohol, or other addictive behaviors.

Hagedorn and Hirshhorn (2009) and Gass (1991) recommend that therapists using AT activities with recovering populations emphasize the act of asking for help in their facilitation of activities. These authors advise therapists to introduce activities in a way that encourages clients to recognize help as an integral part of both the solution to the activity and their long-term recovery. As discussed above, mutual support is also the cornerstone of peer support groups such as AA.

Since 12 Step fellowships are ubiquitous in the field of addiction recovery, I became curious as to whether and how the 12 Steps themselves could be integrated into ABC programming. I interviewed adventure therapists at several treatment centers about how they employ ABC to treat recovering individuals. Most of the practitioners said that they didn't focus explicitly on specific steps but rather integrated principles underlying the steps into their treatment design, focusing primarily on the principles inherent in Step 1 (accepting one's own powerlessness), Step 2 (coming to believe that receiving help is possible), and Step 3 (asking for or surrendering to the source of that help; Alcoholics Anonymous, 2001/1939).

One particularly poignant example of accepting help was offered by Emily Mattimoe:

> We have a task called Willpower that involves a 20-foot-long very thin cable, and I ask people if they think they can walk across it by themselves. Most people who say they think they can get about halfway across usually make it three or four feet before they fall off, and they try again and again, until they are finally ready to accept some additional support. At that point, I offer them just one little finger, and that makes all the difference. They make it all the way across, every time. A lot of times there is help available but we never want to take it. By offering them that tiny little finger they get to experience what a difference even a tiny bit of support can make. It gets them talking about their fear of admitting that they can't do something on their own.

This vignette offers a powerful example of how ABC can impart vital tenets of recovery in ways that merely talking about them cannot—in this case, asking for help, which is the critical tenet of the first three steps.

Because willpower is generally insufficient to combat addiction, it is assumed that recovering individuals need to partner with a benevolent force *outside themselves* in order to maintain sobriety. The notion of a higher power, a potential force other than one's own will, is central to 12 Step recovery. In AA parlance, that power is said to be a loving God of one's own understanding, but it can be any helping entity, including a therapy group.

Deana Grall uses an activity called Blind Vision to help her patients access their non-cognitive, intuitive abilities, which for many people gives access to their higher power. As she describes it, in Blind Vision, a tree with a ribbon tied around it is designated the collective higher power for the group. The group members are blindfolded near the tree and then escorted some distance away from it. They are told that their challenge is to find that very tree again without using their eyes. Deana said that those who try to locate the tree through memory, counting steps, or other cognitive problem-solving skills almost invariably have more difficulty successfully completing their search than those who rely on their intuition alone. As participants practice trusting their intuition, they become able to surrender to their higher power.

Members of 12-step programs are advised to thoroughly work through the steps with a sponsor. Whereas self-help group meetings provide a sense of community for recovering individuals, the steps provide a guide to developing and maintaining a sober life. Some of the steps can be quite laborious and even intimidating, and working through them can take weeks or months. Others are not as time-consuming, but their cerebral nature and emphasis on a "higher power" can be an impediment for those who identify as atheistic or agnostic. ABC offers a tangible experience of a higher power through the collective, visceral energy of the whole group.

In building upon the work of others (Horne, 1997; Gass, 1995), I developed an ABC program called Recovery Adventure Day (RAD). RAD employs structured activities that offer an enjoyable and stimulating approach to engaging in all twelve of AA's steps, usually within a single day. The next chapter describes the ABC activities that I use to help patients work through the 12 Steps by capturing the essence of each of the steps through various problem-solving challenges. Note that while AA's 12 Steps refer specifically to alcohol, the 12 Step approach can be and frequently is applied to the treatment of other substance use disorders and process addictions. RAD offers a sampling of the steps in a package that most people find easy to assimilate. It is not meant to serve as a replacement for working through the steps with a sponsor, but it does offer an enjoyable way to experience the spirit of recovery—namely, the ability to engage in life in a happy, playful, and focused manner without resorting to addictive behavior.

Chapter Eighteen

Recovery Adventure Day

Recovery Adventure Day (RAD) provides a unique way for group members to experience the principles embedded in the 12 Steps of Alcoholics Anonymous. The activities in this chapter are specifically geared to accommodate the setting of a typical treatment center. The activities can be done in a large group room or in an outdoor setting, weather and other circumstances permitting. Before delving into the activities, I usually begin with a few warm-up exercises that set a playful tone for the day. These warm-up activities are intended to foster an atmosphere of positive risk-taking in which adopting new behaviors is supported.

Please note that in some instances I refer the reader to explanations of the activities in part II of this book, and I add context in this chapter for processing the activities specifically with recovering individuals. In other instances, the explanation for an activity presented earlier in the text is repeated here so as to make all the activities easily accessible.

WARM-UP ACTIVITIES

Chiji Card Check-In

Materials Needed: A deck of Chiji playing cards (available online)
Approximate Time: A couple of minutes per group member
Description: A deck of Chiji cards depicts 52 unique, colorful images that evoke a variety of archetypes, locations, and objects. Arrange the chairs of your group members in a semicircle and spread the Chiji cards face-up on the floor in front of the group. Ask each of your group members to select one to three cards that help describe (1) their current mood, (2) a goal they have for the day, and (3) something they would like to share about themselves

with other members of the group. This simple check-in activity immediately establishes that you will be applying metaphorical thinking throughout the day. Simply invite each person to share what cards they selected and talk about why the particular cards appealed to them.

Processing Points: Did group members find points of connection between each other through the cards that were selected? How did people choose what to share about themselves? What level of risk was assumed? This might be a good opportunity to talk about how perceived risk is part of the methodology of ABC.

Stretching

Materials Needed: None
Approximate Time: 5 minutes
Description: I like to start RAD with some simple stretching. I ask one person to demonstrate and lead a stretch that others are invited to follow. The person in the middle continues to model a stretch until another group member says the phrase "I'd like to make a change." That person then switches places with the person in the middle of the circle and leads a different stretch until yet another person volunteers to go in the middle by announcing that they'd "like to make a change." After a few people have had a turn leading, I challenge those who have not taken a turn yet to do so. Some people will say that they can't think of a stretch. I then explain that the stretching part is less important than their willingness to state that they'd like to make a change. I leave time for everyone to step into the middle, but I do not insist that they do so.

Processing Points: Give your group members an opportunity to talk about what it felt like to take ownership of the decision to make a change. If you are working with people in early to middle recovery, some of them are likely to be in treatment at the request of a loved one or an authority figure. They may or may not have internalized the decision to make a major life change. I usually take this opportunity to talk about the importance of internalizing the decision to recover. I explain that it's fine to start recovery at someone else's urging, but in order for long-term recovery to stick, the decision to change needs to come from within. Sometimes this can prompt an honest discussion about group members' ambivalence about being in treatment. This is an important topic to have out in the open and available for reflection.

Puzzle Pairs

Materials Needed: A Rhyming Words set. Rhyming Words is a children's game that includes pairs of words on puzzle pieces (available online, in many toy stores, and as part of the RAD kit).

Approximate Time: 10 minutes

Description: The game set consists of 48 puzzle pieces. As the name implies, each puzzle piece has a word on it that rhymes with a word on another piece, making 24 rhyming pairs total. In addition to depicting words that rhyme, each pair fits snugly together and has matching background colors. For example, the background color for the Flag and Bag puzzle pieces are the same. Count out one puzzle piece for each group member, ensuring that everyone has a match. Include yourself if you have an odd number in your group. It's important that each person has a puzzle piece that pairs with another group member's piece.

Explain that you are going to hand a puzzle piece to each group member, *but they should not look at it!* Each person should hold their puzzle piece face-down so that they can see only the back of the puzzle piece (all of the backs of the pieces are identical). Next, say that you would like everyone to hold their puzzle piece face-out, away from them, so that others can see the image but each person cannot see their own. Say that the task is for everyone to find their partner. Your group members may be puzzled by this direction. That is okay. It should quickly become evident that they need to rely on one another in order to be successful. Group members can ask each other for clarification about what is on their puzzle pieces. Some will take the initiative and start pointing others in the direction of their partner. Some will experiment with trial and error, simply trying to find a physical match for their piece. This is okay, but the preferred method here is relying on others' direction. You can wander around the room and let the pairs know when they have been successful. If not, they can continue to search for their partner.

Processing Points: Ask your group members how they were able to be successful. What feelings arose in them when they realized that they needed to accept the guidance of others in order to succeed? Is there shame in accepting support? Were group members more focused on assisting others or finding their own partner? Is this a pattern that is familiar to them? There are many ways in which the puzzle pairs match. Name these aloud and ask your participants to name other ways in which they might find points of connection with each other.

Part 2 (optional): After all the pairs have been identified, ask each pair to create a sentence that includes both their words. They will then recite the sentence aloud for the group. They can recite the sentence in unison, or they can divide it up in any way they like. For example, they might choose to have one person say the first half of the sentence and the other person say the second half, or one could recite the whole sentence while the other acts it out. In other words, they have a license to be creative. Give the group a minute or two to rehearse, and then ask for a volunteer to start. Give each pair an opportunity to perform their sentence.

Processing Points: Give your group members an opportunity to reflect on how they collaborated with their partner. Did one person assume the lead while the other went along with whatever was suggested? Even with a simple task like composing a sentence, social roles begin to emerge. Ask whether the roles assumed during the activity were similar to roles that the participants take on in other contexts. Also, if your group members were laughing during the activity, ask how it felt to allow themselves to be playful with each other. Say that although recovery is serious business, you hope that they can experience a shared sense of play with you during the day.

Knee Tag

Materials Needed: A stopwatch or timer
Approximate Time: 5 minutes
Description: This activity helps to establish a norm of taking acceptable risks and trying new things. The trickiest part of Knee Tag is explaining it. Ask your group members to stand with their hands covering their knees. Explain that they can only move when their hands are off of their knees. Instruct them to remove their hands from their knees and take few steps, and then cover their knees and freeze. Repeat this process several times. Next, explain that they will try to *gently* tag each other's knees as many times as they can within a 45-second period that you will time. One point is awarded for each knee that is tagged. Each person should keep track of their own score. The key factor here is that the only way to get points is by making oneself vulnerable since one's knees necessarily need to be uncovered if one is to move or tag someone else.

Play one round and ask your group members to comment on the quality with which they played. Most groups will be cautious the first time through. Challenge your group members to take more risks the second time they play.

Processing Points: Discuss the difference between the real and perceived risk entailed in being vulnerable. What does it mean to be vulnerable? What is the emotional equivalent of "uncovering one's knees" during group therapy sessions? Why is this risky, and what have been people's actual experiences when they took such risks? Did they get injured? What steps might we take in life if we allowed ourselves to assume a little more emotional risk?

STEP 1

*We admitted we were powerless over alcohol—that our lives
had become unmanageable.*

The key words in this step are *powerless* and *unmanageable*. It's important to find activities that engender a sense of chaos, the experience of actions occurring that are clearly beyond personal control or an experience of defeat that requires outside assistance to recover from. A classic ABC intervention known as The Maze (see below) offers most participants a very powerful reflection on their attitude toward asking for help. I have also found tag games in which many people can be "It" useful for capturing the essence of Step 1. For smaller groups, Joined at the Wrists (see below) offers another experience of powerlessness and the need to ask for assistance.

STEP 1 ACTIVITIES

Amoeba Tag

Materials Needed: A very soft throwable object such as a squishy ball, and a playing area of at least 20×30 feet

Approximate Time: 5 minutes

Description: As the name implies, Amoeba Tag results in all players eventually being absorbed by an ever-growing Amoeba. An approximately 20×30 foot playing area is delineated. If playing outdoors, you can use pylons or other boundary markers. If playing indoors, clear any furniture to the sides of the room, and the four walls can function as your boundaries. One player begins by being designated "It." It starts targeting others by tossing the soft, squishy ball at them. As each person is hit by the squishy object, he or she becomes frozen from the waist down and immediately becomes part of the Amoeba team. The frozen Its may toss the ball to each other, in effect becoming an It team, but they cannot move from where each of them is standing. The facilitator can retrieve the ball and hand it back to a member of the Amoeba. No matter how fast or crafty someone is, eventually the inevitable will happen and they will be absorbed into the ever-expanding blob. You can play a couple of rounds with the last person moving in each round starting the Amoeba for the following round.

Processing Points: In addition to providing an apt metaphor for the experience of powerlessness, this activity makes for a rousing warm-up activity early in a program. You can talk about where else in life your group members have experienced a sense of inevitability.

The Maze, or No Way Out

Materials Needed: One blindfold or bandana for each group member and enough rope to define the circumference of a playing area large enough for your group members to walk around in. For a group of up to 12 participants, an area approximately 12×15 feet should be about right. You will also need relatively stable and heavy items to anchor the ropes. If you're working in an outdoor setting, trees will do beautifully. When you're indoors, rectangular tables turned up on their narrow ends work well, as do structural pillars. If your work environment permits it, you can anchor heavy eyebolts at various spots around the circumference of the room and run the ropes through the eyebolts. Long bungee cords work well for opening and closing the entrance to the playing area as they can be faster to work with than rope, which needs to be tied and untied.

Approximate Time: 30 minutes

Description: The Maze is an activity I also like to call "No Way Out," which better captures the fatalistic inevitability of untreated addiction. Gass, Gillis, and Russell (2012) use this activity to illustrate how ABC can be applied to recovery from addiction. As mentioned above, the activity can be facilitated indoors or outside. The Maze, unlike most of the activities in this book, requires advance setup. When working outdoors, you should have no problem setting up well in advance. You'll want to find several trees that can encompass an area approximately 12×15 feet (smaller for small groups and maybe a little bigger for groups of more than 12). Ideally, the activity will have been set up so that the participants will not have seen it before they experience it. When working indoors, the element of surprise can be harder to achieve. When I have facilitated full-day, recovery-oriented programs, I have set this activity up during lunch and requested that the group members gather in an adjacent room to start the afternoon session. If you have the luxury of a room you can dedicate to this one activity, you can set up before the program begins. If you have an assistant, the activity can probably be set up during a 10- or 15-minute break. Just ask your participants to meet just outside the door to the room.

The trickiest part of this activity is leading your group members into the playing area because in order for the activity to be successful, the participants should not have seen the playing area before they enter it. I usually ask people to put on their blindfolds and then join hands as I lead them into the roped-off area. Once all group members are inside, the "entrance" to the roped-off area needs to be closed using a piece of rope or similar material. If you have a co-facilitator, they can guide people who are toward the back of the line.

Next, the therapist explains to the group members that their task is to find their way out of the roped-off area. However, they may not climb over or duck under any of the ropes or manipulate them in any way. If time and materials permit, I suggest wrapping the playing area at least twice all the way around. This makes it very clear where the boundaries are. Explain that once someone has found their way out, you will remove their blindfold, and from that point on, the player will be able to observe from outside the playing area, but they should remain silent.

The "way out" is not a physical solution but rather a willingness to ask for help. The group leader needs to listen carefully for any expression of asking for help. The most obvious of these might be "I need help" or "Can someone please get me out of here?" It's up to the group leader to discern if help is being asked for. If so, the person's blindfold is removed by the facilitator and the player is nonverbally directed to exit the playing area. At this point ducking under the rope is fine. The facilitator can lift the rope temporarily to indicate that the person may now exit the maze. As the group gradually decreases in size, those left in the middle become increasingly aware that there is in fact a way out; it's just not a physical opening as they had ima-gined.

Processing Points: This activity serves as a potent reflection on the par-ticipants' ability or inability to ask for and accept help. It can be a very painful experience for those left wandering around looking for a physical exit. I usually set a time limit of about 30 minutes because the point has usually been made by then. Anecdotally, in mixed-gender groups, it is often men who are the last remaining group members. You can talk about how men are conditioned not to ask for help and how this can be an impediment in some situations. Take time to let people talk about their emotional reactions to this activity. Those who got out early, for example, will have had a chance to empathize with those who remained in the maze longer. Be sure to make the analogy to each group member's process of asking for help to recover from their addiction. How long did they remain in "the roped-off area" of their addiction before surrendering to the need for assistance?

There is some semantic trickery involved in the setup of this activity since most people will think of physical solutions when the group leader explains that there is a way out of the maze. So the way people relate to language may influence the way they interpret the directions. As a result, some negative feelings toward the group leader might be generated by this activity. Allow those feelings to surface and be freely expressed. Emotional freedom is a key to successful recovery.

> During a multi-family ABC program, the primary patients had had a lot of experience taking in help and support, so they were among the first out of the maze. The patients' fathers were among the last in the maze, circling around endlessly as they were determined to find their own way out. This experience allowed the primary

Looking for a way out. *Photo by Ben Silverman.*

patients to emerge as leaders in their families, which made for a nice antidote to having been seen as the problem family member during their active addiction.

Source: Gass, 1995.

Joined at the Wrists (aka Handcuffs)

Materials Needed: For each two group members, two 3-foot lengths of rope of different colors with a slip knot and loop at each end of each rope. For a group of 12, you might use six green rope lengths and six yellow rope lengths, for example. If you don't have that much rope, it's also fine to allow group members to alternate participating and observing.

Description: For each pair of group members who are participating, place two chairs opposite each other about three feet apart. Explain that you are going to join the two group members together using the lengths of rope. One person puts the loops of one of the ropes around each of his or her wrists and then makes sure that the slipknots are snug around the wrists but not too tight. The second rope gets passed behind the opposing rope before it is similarly attached to the second participant's wrists.

Explain that the task is for the two participants to find a way to become free of each other *without manipulating the slipknots.* They need to be completely disentangled so that each could walk to a different corner of the room

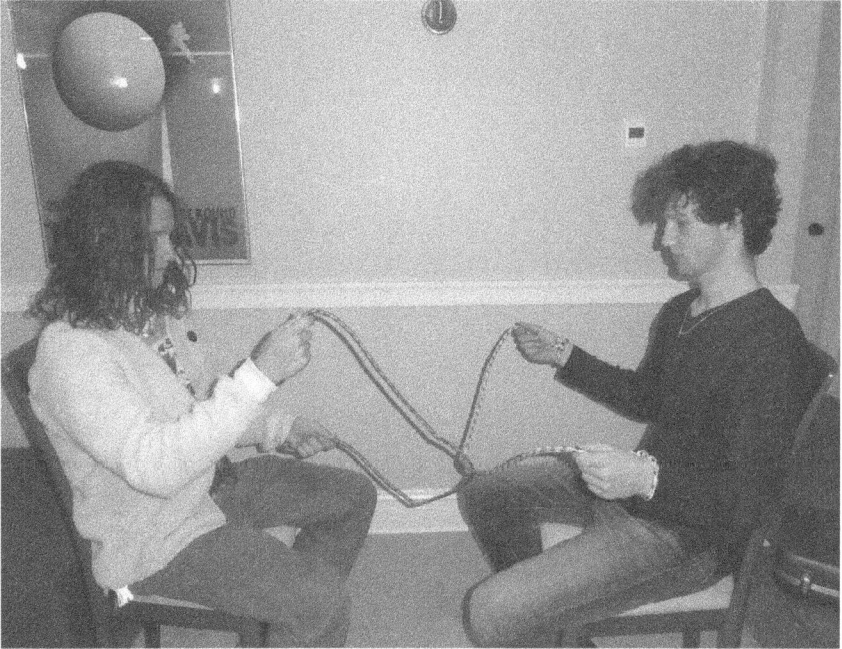

Joined at the Wrists setup. *Photo by the author.*

if they wanted to. The key here is that neither person can remove their wrists from the loops. Most pairs will spin around multiple times before they become ready to ask for assistance. After all, this task is designed to create a feeling of powerlessness. In very rare instances, participants who have not previously seen the activity or are not experts in knots and ropes will find their way out without assistance. Allow the pairs to struggle as long as they are willing to. As with other activities described in this book, you want to facilitate a frustration level that is therapeutic and intentional and not one just to make people squirm.

The key to emancipation here is for one person to pinch a looped section of his or her own rope and pass it *under* the bottom of the loop around his or her counterpart's wrist (let's call this a bracelet). This newly formed loop should be pulled through the bottom of the partner's "bracelet" from behind (from the elbow end of the hand toward the fingertips), and then up and over the partner's hand. After having been passed through in this manner, the loop should then pass *under* the top of the partner's bracelet, and "Presto!" the couple is free. This process can be tricky at first, so allow yourself plenty of time to practice so that you can then share the solution with your group members.

Discovering a solution! *Photo by the author.*

Processing Points: How long did your group members struggle before they became willing to ask for help? How did this process compare to their being in active addiction before becoming willing to surrender and accept support to move in a different direction? What feelings arose in your group members when they realized that they might need some assistance? Is asking for help shameful for some people? What lessons about asking for help did your group members learn in their families and in school?

Note: Be aware that the process of literally being tied up can kindle traumatic memories for some people. Some may associate it with being held against their will or even with being arrested. Some people may choose to observe at first. Allow them to do so.

Texts and Emails (aka Phones and Faxes)

Materials Needed: One soft throwable object per group member. I suggest using the "water bomb" balls that can be purchased at most dollar stores, though water is not used during the activity.

Approximate Time: 10 minutes

Description: Ask your group members to stand in a circle with one person standing in the middle. Everyone in the outer circle has a soft ball of some kind that cannot cause injury. The person in the center counts "One, two, three!" and on "three!" everyone tosses their ball toward him or her. The person in the center tries to catch as many of the balls as they can. The balls should be tossed underhanded so that they fly with an arc, making it as easy as possible for the person in the center to catch them. I usually demonstrate by being in the middle first so that group members can see there is no shame in catching only one or even none of the balls. After demonstrating, give everyone who wants to be in the middle a turn. Then, after they all have experienced the unmanageability of the task, ask if they can think of any alternative ways of going about the task so that the person in the middle can be more successful. Usually someone will think of pairing up with another group member or working in a small group, which becomes a metaphor for recovery. Another option might be using a piece of clothing to catch the balls—the garment then becomes a metaphor for a tool of recovery such as a sponsor or inspirational reading material. The two rules that need to remain in place are that all the balls need to be launched at the same time and that the group members should remain standing in a circle.

Processing Points: After drawing a connection between this activity and group members' addictions, you can take time to discuss other areas of people's lives in which they experience powerlessness. Because accepting help by partnering with others or using available resources is a key to success during this activity, it makes for a fitting transition to Step 2, which involves coming to believe in a power greater than oneself. In the case of this activity, that power becomes other people and resources—all things "greater than," or in addition to, oneself.

Note that this activity also appears in chapter 7, along with a photo.

Source: Rohnke, 1984.

STEP 2

*Came to believe that a Power greater than ourselves
could restore us to sanity.*

One of the reasons that this step is elusive to many people is that they miss the nuance in the idea that *coming to believe* may be a gradual process. Newcomers to AA are sometimes put off by the mistaken notion that they must experience a total and instantaneous religious conversion. Not so. For Step 2, I favor activities that by their very nature cannot be accomplished by one person acting alone. The process of accomplishing a task by joining with others tends to bring about a belief in a power greater than oneself—namely, the group itself!

STEP 2 ACTIVITIES

All Touch

Materials Needed: One empty can (a 4-oz. can for groups of 20 or more will work well, and smaller cans or other objects will work for smaller groups). I have used the top of a dry erase marker for groups of eight to 12 with good results. A thimble also works well for smaller groups.

Approximate Time: 5 minutes

Description: This simple activity involves asking everyone in the group to make physical contact with an object *without making contact with each other*. Obviously, the smaller the object, the greater the challenge. Adjust the object size according to number of participants. I usually start by placing the object on the ground and then describing the challenge. The group may soon discover that they need to pick the object up in order to proceed. I do not tell them this, though they might ask me if they can pick the object up. "Yes" is the answer to that question.

Processing Points: There are opportunities here to talk about making sacrifices on behalf of the group. Did specific group members make helpful

From "That's impossible" to "We did it!" *Photo by the author.*

contributions? What factors contributed to the group's success? What roles emerged during the activity?

> I presented this challenge to a group of 12 people who were early in their recovery from addictive disorders. Some group members were meeting each other for the first time during the ABC session with me, so the sense of newness was amplified (new group, new modality, and new way of life). I put a small rock on the ground that was about the size of the top of an adult's thumb, and then I explained the challenge. I heard more than one person say, "That's impossible" or "You have to be kidding." About two minutes later, the group had accomplished the task! The experience of moving from "That's impossible" to "We did it!" was memorable and easily transferable to the process of recovery from addiction, which can seem impossible at times to those early in the process.

Note that this activity is also described in chapter 5.

Source: Rohnke, 1984.

Tennis Ball Transfer (aka Bull Ring)

Materials Needed: One tennis ball, two stands on which the tennis ball can rest, and a 2-inch metal ring with eight 10-foot lengths of string attached to it, which will be used to transport the ball from one stand to the other. The stands can be constructed out of PVC pipe. The ball will balance nicely atop a 1-inch-diameter piece of PVC pipe. This upright "stand" needs to be stabilized by another length of PVC pipe and a connector, or you can make a wooden stand that a length of PVC pipe has been attached to. The metal ring should fit easily over the stand, with the tennis ball placed on top.

Approximate Time: 15 minutes

Description: There are many challenges that can be used to evoke an experience of joining. One that works especially well is Tennis Ball Transfer, aka Bull Ring. Each group member holds one length of string as close to the end as possible, but not more than six inches from the end. If you have fewer people in a group, some can hold the ends of two lengths of string, while others hold just one. The ring is placed over a stand made of PVC pipe. Position another stand about 40 feet away from the first. The challenge is for the group to transport the tennis ball from one stand to the other, holding only the ends of the strings. If the ball falls to the ground, the group starts over. With larger groups, two subgroups can cross while simultaneously moving the balls to opposite stands. A "safe landing" means that the ball remains on the stand for at least 10 seconds after the group members have all let go of their strings. You can have fun dividing the group into two using some of the questions provided in the Take a Stand activity described in chapter 14 and in Step 4, just ahead.

A test of group members' patience—practice makes improvement. *Photo by the author.*

The level of challenge during this activity can be modulated by changing the type of ball that is used. For example, a golf ball's weight and density will decrease the level of difficulty whereas using a Whiffle ball will increase it. For most groups, a tennis ball provides the right degree of challenge.

Processing Points: This activity is useful for assessing emergent leadership and other roles within a group. To be successful, every participant needs to remain focused on the task. I recommend taking time after the activity to reflect on these dynamics with your group members. Where else in life do they use a high level of focus and in what areas would they like to become more focused? How does being a leader or a follower serve them in other domains? Was there a saboteur in the group? How did that person develop a tendency to take on a destructive role? Also, if the ball fell repeatedly, there could be an opportunity to reflect on how group members tolerated frustration. Did they look for someone to blame when the ball fell?

> I was working with a group that encountered a high level of frustration during Tennis Ball Transfer. After struggling for over 45 minutes to complete the task, one group member said that she felt like punching one of her peers. This revelation allowed the

two group members to work through some long-festering hostility between them. The frustration experienced during the activity made overt an interpersonal tension that had remained hidden until that point. The two group members experienced a better working relationship in the group as a result of having worked through their differences. This process reduced the tension between them outside the group as well.

Source: Cain and Jolliff, 1998.

Toxic Waste

Materials Needed: One 15-foot length of rope, a rubber bracelet such as those used for social movements such as the Livestrong campaign, several 5-foot pieces of string, a tennis ball with a face drawn on it, and a receptacle such as a tin can that is large enough to hold the tennis ball.

Approximate Time: 15 minutes

Description: Make a loose circle on the floor out of the length of rope and place the tennis ball and the tin can on the floor in the middle of the circle. Explain that "Tennie" has found herself in a dangerous situation. She is traveling and has found herself in an area that is full of bars and business acquaintances who love to drink. She needs to get to an AA meeting, which is represented by the tin can. However, it would be far too dangerous for any of the group members to venture into that territory by themselves. They may, however, use the materials on hand to help get Tennie to the meeting. For their own safety, group members may not enter the roped-off area or make contact with it at all (Toxic Waste also appears in chapter 5, where you'll find a depiction of the setup).

Processing Points: The discussion points applicable to Tennis Ball Transfer, described above, can be applied to this activity. What was it like to realize that no one person could accomplish the task alone and that joining with others was required? Are your group members "coming to believe that a power greater than themselves" (i.e., the group) can restore them to sanity?

This activity provides an opportunity to talk about what potentially slippery situations your group members are likely to find themselves in during early recovery. How might they prepare for the tests that will inevitably arise as they transition from treatment into living a sober, productive life? What resources will they use to help them get though these tests with their sobriety intact?

STEP 3

Made a decision to turn our will and our lives
over to the care of God as we understood Him.

This step is another one that is often confusing to newcomers to recovery, especially those who do not believe in a traditional God. The spirituality embedded in AA is frequently mistaken for religiosity, which is then off-putting to many people who may identify as secular. The word "God" is mentioned numerous times in the Steps, and that in itself is often experienced as an impediment to recovery for atheists or those who are otherwise averse to a traditional view of God. Nowhere does this issue become more apparent than in Step 3.

For RAD, I conceptualize this "higher power" as the group itself, and I select activities for RAD that are designed to foster interdependence among group members. The active part of Step 3 is *making a decision* to turn one's will and life over to the care of a loving, benevolent force outside oneself. I have found that trust-building activities offer group members a powerful kinesthetic experience of making such a decision.

STEP 3 ACTIVITIES

Trust Leans

Materials Needed: None
Approximate Time: 10 minutes
Description: Trust Leans are done in pairs. They work best when partners of approximately equal height and weight work together. Before attempting a lean, each pair should practice "spotting" technique, and they need to learn a series of rote phrases, as follows:

Leaner: "Spotter ready?"
Spotter: "Ready."
Leaner: "Ready to lean."
Spotter: "Lean on."

After everyone has mastered the dialogue above, the group needs to learn the correct positions for leaning and spotting. Spotting position is one foot back and two hands facing up and out at chest height, so as to create a springy cushion for the person leaning. The leaner should keep his or her body erect (no bending at the knees or hips, and keep the back straight) and cross their arms over their chest. The spotter should stand with their hands about six to 12 inches from the leaner's shoulders. The commands should be said aloud, and when the leaner hears "Lean on," he or she leans backward and allows the spotter to catch them. Invite the pair to repeat the process before changing roles, this time with the spotter allowing the leaner to fall a little bit farther.

Bookends is a Trust Lean with three people, a spotter on each side of the leaner. The same pattern of communication is used as in Trust Leans, only

Ready to lean. *Photo by the author.*

the plural is used ("Spotters ready?"). The person leaning allows him- or herself to be gently tipped backward and forward between the spotters.

Willow in the Wind requires a group of at least eight participants who all assume spotting positions in a tight circle while one person stands in the center with their arms crossed. The person in the center allows themselves to be gently supported and tipped in different directions within the circle. With adequate spotting, the person has an experience of being "held" and supported by the group. By surrendering their self-sufficiency, they can enjoy the powerful support available in the group. The same phrases can be used for Willow in the Wind as in Bookends.

Willow in the Wind can be used diagnostically with a group as it provides a gauge of a group's ability to focus and support one another. If pushing and subterfuge occurs, that tells me I need to progress slowly with that particular group. (See the second figure in chapter 2.)

Processing Points: Trust activities tend to bring up a lot of feelings. Most people experience some fear. Ideally this is just a momentary uncertainty about whether or not the spotter will be there for them. The experience of being gently caught and supported can be corrective for people who have experienced abandonment in their lives.

Lean on. *Photo by the author.*

I suggest that group members be prompted to think about whether they were more comfortable in the spotting or leaning role. The spotter is in greater control during this activity, so a strong preference for the spotting role may indicate a need to be in control. For others in recovery, falling might feel more familiar and comfortable as they may have been uncomfortable taking on responsibility in their lives.

Since all these activities involve touch, they might be especially threatening to people who have been victims of physical or sexual abuse. The activities provide an opportunity for group members to talk about what it means to experience contact in a safe and supportive environment. Thus, this series of trust activities can function as a corrective experience.

The analogy for Step 3 is pretty clear here as the leaners are momentarily turning their life over to the care of the group. This allows them a tangible doorway to experiencing a reliance on a power outside of ("greater than") themselves.

Trust Webbing Circle

Materials Needed: One 15-foot length of 1-inch nylon webbing, available at most outdoor-oriented stores. The piece of webbing should be made into a large loop with a water knot. The more pressure put on a water knot, the tighter it gets, so you can feel secure that the knot will not become undone during the activity.

Approximate Time: 10 minutes

Description: With your group members standing in a circle, ask them to hold onto the webbing with two hands as if they were water-skiing. Explain that in a moment you are going to ask them to keep their bodies straight like a board as they slowly lean back with their arms straight out and allow themselves to be supported by the whole group. Access the group's stability, and provided that they are relatively stable, invite all the group members to take a baby step toward the center of the circle. This will initiate more mutual support and greater reliance on the group to support each of its members.

In the event that the group starts to lose its balance, ask everyone to take a step back and support themselves as they regroup and prepare to begin anew. Ask if the group members want to reposition themselves so as to create a more even distribution of weight around the circle. Allow enough attempts so that the group gets to experience a prolonged moment during which each of

Mutual support in action. *Photo by Ben Silverman.*

the group members is truly allowing the group to support them. As this is happening, I will often comment on the collective power in the group. I invite my group members to breathe deeply and appreciate the abundance of support that is available to them.

Processing Points: People usually have a powerful response to this activity. What feelings are aroused in your group members as they attempt this challenge? Are these feelings familiar to those they associate with asking for and accepting support? Offer your group members an opportunity to talk about their prior experiences of either having been supported or "dropped" through parental neglect or unwanted criticism. How might these prior experiences be impacting their ability to accept consistent support now? Be aware that this question can prompt some emotionally evocative material. Allow enough time for your group members to talk at length about these issues, if they seem primed to do so, or make a verbal note that you will revisit this topic during another group session.

Note: Though I have never seen anyone injured while attempting this activity, it does involve some degree of risk. Due to the pressure put on people's shoulders, those with arm or shoulder injuries should probably observe. If you have extra staff on hand, they can assume spotting positions behind different quadrants of the group. While the actual risk of anyone falling backward is very low, the perceived risk during this activity is significant, so the presence of spotters may be reassuring to some.

Source: Cain and Smith, 2002.

STEP 4

Made a searching and fearless moral inventory of ourselves.

For those involved in "working the steps" of AA, Step Four is generally the most time-consuming and laborious of all the steps. The recovering individual is often advised to fill the pages of a notebook with the names of everyone they have ever wronged and anyone for whom they have developed a resentment. Likewise, all of a person's fears are often recorded as well. These emotional liabilities are counterbalanced by listing the person's positive attributes as well. While there are many approaches to completing Step Four, all of them involve a good deal of self-reflection. I use sociometric exercises to give participants a taste of the breadth of self-contemplation the fourth step calls for. My favorite of these exercises is known as Take a Stand, or Continuum, which was described in chapter 14 and will be expanded upon here.

STEP 4 ACTIVITIES

Take a Stand (aka Continuum)

Materials Needed: None

Approximate Time: 10–15 minutes

Description: In this exercise taken from the practice of sociometry, participants are invited to reflect on and disclose various preferences and attributes about themselves according to where they choose to literally stand on a continuum that is defined by the facilitator. For example, you might delineate "the end of the room with the door" and the "end of the room with the clock" as the two ends of the playing area, each representing an extreme of the criteria being presented. The facilitator then describes a series of opposing qualities, and the group members position themselves along the continuum according to their preference, or how they might assess themselves. Group members are free to stand anywhere along the continuum as most of the categories are not either-or propositions but rather questions of degree or preference. Some of the questions force a clear choice, but most of them offer room for interpretation and invite self-reflection. The topics become increasingly personal as the exercise progresses, and therefore disclosure grows increasingly risky. For the purposes of Step 4, I start with some general questions and then move into content that would constitute a "moral inventory," as is mentioned in the step. In cases in which the criteria could be interpreted any number of ways, I provide some additional criteria, indicated in parentheses below. I encourage my group members to move through the following sequence with a spirit of curiosity and a nonjudgmental attitude toward themselves and others. After all, most of our attributes have some advantages and some challenges associated with them. For example, being more focused on others than ourselves may indicate altruistic tendencies, but it can result in one not getting their own needs met and then developing resentment. Many people who fall prey to addiction grew up in families where addiction was present (Black, 1981; Roth, 2004). Family members of addicts often have great difficulty focusing on their own needs. The central directive of Al-Anon, a fellowship for loved ones of alcoholics, is to "keep the focus on ourselves and not on the alcoholic." Because alcoholics often engender fear and worry in their family members, the family members can become preoccupied with the addict and lose touch with their own thoughts, feelings, and needs. In addition, many of us learn that it is selfish to focus on oneself and noble to attend to the needs of others. Many people who end up in treatment settings are overdue to focus on their own thoughts and feelings. Ultimately, we want to support people we work with in finding balance between focusing on themselves and being present for others.

Here are some criteria you might want to use for this activity.

1. Are you a morning person or a night owl? (Morning people tend to be most productive earlier in the day while night owls get increasingly energetic and creative during the evening hours.)
2. Cross your arms. Is the left or right elbow on top?
3. Interlock your fingers. Is the left or right thumb on top? (Changing a habit can be difficult, even something as simple as how we cross our fingers. Encourage your group members to be patient with themselves as they learn to live in a new way.)
4. Do you believe that nature or nurture is more telling in shaping us? ("Nature" refers to our genetic make-up, whereas "nurture" concerns the environment in which we were raised.)
5. Are you a head-centered or heart-centered person? (Head-centered people are very analytical. They routinely do cost-benefit comparisons and try to weigh the advantages and drawbacks of a given situation before making any decision. Heart-centered people tend to go with their intuition, or "gut-feeling," and don't deliberate much before moving into action.)
6. Are you an introvert or an extrovert? (Introverts get a sense of renewal from reading, taking a long walk, or meditating, while extroverts get their batteries recharged by going to a social event and interacting with others.)
7. Are you a tortoise or a hare? (Tortoises are methodical. They read all the directions before starting assembly, and they really take their time. Hares try to get ten things accomplished before lunch. They are very energetic, bordering on frenetic.)
8. Are you trusting or mistrustful when meeting new people?
9. Are you resentful or free of resentment?
10. Are you self-focused or primarily interested in others? (At first, we might think it is noble to be interested in others, but being exclusively "other-focused" can be a detriment if it comes at the expense of neglecting one's own needs. It's important to think of both ourselves and others.)
11. Do you believe in a higher power or not?
12. Are you generous or stingy?
13. Are you truthful or do you put on airs?
14. Are you judgmental or accepting of others?
15. Are you self-accepting or critical of yourself?

Processing Points: Inevitably, the last pair of questions prompts people to reveal that they are more critical and less accepting of themselves than they are of others. This offers an opportunity to ask why most of us are tougher on ourselves than we are on others. Even imagining becoming more self-accepting might constitute a step in that direction. You can also ask how it felt to share information about oneself in a group context. How was this different from or similar to what happens during group therapy? Participants will often say that the fact that everyone was in it together made the activity seem inviting and not so threatening.

Feel free to pause between questions if you notice something striking or unusual about a particular group, or if your group members feel motivated to share after each round. For example, when working with people in recovery, it is not uncommon to have most of your group members identify themselves as more on the extroverted side. Research has shown that extroverts are more susceptible to addiction than their introverted counterparts (Cain, 2012). If and when this occurs, you can explain that extroverted people often have a higher tolerance for stimulation and so for that reason alone are more vulnerable to addiction than their introverted counterparts. Becoming aware of this correlation might result in increased self-compassion for your participants.

Fears Inventory

Materials Needed: A set of index cards with a fear and its definition written on each one. I suggest writing the fears in bold letters with a marker and using a finer point to write in the definitions below each word.

Approximate Time: 30 minutes

Description: Listing all of one's fears is often incorporated as part of working the fourth step. The value of doing so may be that unless one's fears are acknowledged and openly shared, they fester and become an underlying cause of a person's returning to addictive behavior as a misguided attempt to reduce their internal fears.

This activity is less active than most in RAD, and so, in addition to prompting some meaningful, fear-reducing sharing, it offers a temporary reprieve from physical activity. The process can be done seated in chairs placed in a circle, or you can invite your group members to sit on the floor and gather around the index cards that you have scattered in the center of the group. Invite your group members to peruse the various fears and then select one that pertains to them that they can then talk about with the group. After each person shares about their fear, offer others an opportunity to identify with that person. It is okay for two or more people to share a card or a fear. There are enough to go around!

Some of the fears I have used include the following:

acrophobia (fear of heights)
anuptiphobia (fear of staying single)
apiphobia (fear of bees)
arachnophobia (fear of spiders)
belenophobia (fear of needles)
claustrophobia (fear of confined spaces)

coulrophobia (fear of clowns)
decidophobia (fear of making decisions)
dentophobia (fear of dentists)
enochlophobia (fear of crowds)
ergophobia (fear of work)
gerascophobia (fear of growing old)
hydrophobia (fear of water)
iatrophobia (fear of doctors)
lygophobia (fear of darkness)
monophobia (fear of being alone)
pyrophobia (fear of fire)
steriophobia (fear of depending on others)
technophobia (fear of technology)
testophobia (fear of tests)
thanatophobia (fear of death)

Processing Points: How have these various fears impacted your group members? Have their fears prevented them from taking important steps in their personal or professional lives? What price have they paid for having persistent and in many cases irrational fears?

What effect do you think talking about our fears has? Does it make them worse or does it have a diminishing effect? Especially when people are ashamed of their fears, taking about them openly and finding that others share similar concerns is likely to diminish the shame and possibly have an ameliorating effect on the fear as well.

> One recovering intravenous heroin addict shared with the group that he had a fear of needles. However, his need to use heroin forced him to revisit his fear on a daily basis. His fear did not diminish, but his need to use drugs overpowered his phobia. Sharing this paradox with the group gave this individual renewed appreciation for the power his addiction had over him.

At this point in a program, participants may be eager to learn more about you, the facilitator. You might get asked what phobias you identify with. You can use this line of inquiry to deepen your work with the group by considering whether you are aware of any fears or concerns in the moment. For example, you might be concerned about making a poor decision about what activities to facilitate, or there may be dynamics going on in the group that are concerning, such as intense interpersonal conflict between two or more members. Speaking about such present concerns can assist the group in doing reflective work.

Source: Cavert, 2015.

STEP 5

Admitted to God, to ourselves, and to another human being
the exact nature of our wrongs.

This step usually entails a confession-like process whereby the recovering individual discloses the specific nature of his or her misdeeds, especially those related to the addictive behavior. Often people will choose their 12 Step program sponsor, a member of the clergy, a trusted friend, or a therapist to confide in. This process allows the individual to come out of hiding and paves the way for the later steps of making amends for one's wrongs. The context of an ABC program is not conducive to each person sharing a detailed personal history, but it may offer an opportunity for people to name some of their faults and fears and connect with others who identify similarly. I use Mousetraps and Commonalities , respectively, to this end.

STEP 5 ACTIVITIES

Mousetraps

Materials Needed: One blindfold for every pair of group members, at least one mousetrap per group member, plus enough rope to define a rectangular playing area of about 10×20 feet. Please refer to the write-up for this activity in chapter 15 for more details on setting the activity up.

Approximate Time: 5 minutes for each pair of group members

Description: In using Mousetraps to capture the essence of Step 5, I ask group members to endow each mousetrap with a problematic trait or behavioral pattern, something that is referred to as a "character defect" in the parlance of AA. Every group member is invited to name a character defect and assign that quality to one of the traps. Some common defects are self-deprecating thoughts, jealousy, boredom, and impatience. There will likely be more traps than there are people in your group. That's fine. I suggest setting some live traps as your group members name qualities such as selfishness, fear, avoidance, anger, etc. The impression created is that the field of traps represents the collective challenges of the whole group, suggesting that each of us is capable of falling into the various "traps" in recovery unless, of course, we accept some guidance along the way.

Each group member chooses another group member or therapist to verbally guide them through the minefield of character defects while blindfolded. Behaviors such as self-sufficiency, pride, and arrogance can be traps that lead people back into their addictive behaviors. The guide in this activity functions much the same way a sponsor does in 12 Step programs, carefully directing their charge through the 12 Steps and on to continued sobriety. In this activity, the guide directs his blindfolded partner safely though the minefield. After the guide has finished leading his partner though the minefield, he can be invited to choose a guide of his own as he passes through. Walking the minefield without shoes increases the perceived risk of this challenge.

Processing Points: This activity is a great opportunity to talk about how your group members think about selecting a sponsor, and once they have one, how they utilize that person. Advice is only good if the recipient is willing to use it. Invite people to talk about their ambivalence with regard to asking someone to sponsor them. What made following their guide's suggestions easy, and what, if anything, got in the way? What concerns do your group members have about asking someone to be their sponsor? Do they even know how to broach such a question? Sometimes simply getting together to talk is a good start to a more formal relationship.

Source: Sikes, 2003.

Commonalities

Materials Needed: None
Approximate Time: 15 minutes
Description: Commonalities offers an opportunity for group members to discuss a problem area with others who face similar challenges. Small groups are formed according to the "character defect" most group members identify with. To start, ask four different people to whisper a character defect to you. You then ask each person who identified a character defect to occupy a different corner of the playing area; in doing so, the respective corners come to represent four specific liabilities (e.g., selfishness, dishonesty, pride, and jealousy). Others in the group need to discover which defect is represented in each corner of the room. They do this by visiting each corner and inquiring. They then choose one corner to identify with and join that group. I then allow 10–15 minutes for each small group to discuss their shared defect. Feel free to visit and join the various small group discussions. If you have extra rooms available at your site, feel free to use them for the small group discussions. The idea here is to give people an opportunity to talk openly with others who share similar interpersonal challenges.

Processing Points: How did each person decide which small group to join? Was this a difficult or easy decision? What did it feel like to talk openly with others about a personal challenge? What is the potential value of taking these kinds of emotional risks?

STEP 6

Were entirely ready to have God remove all these defects of character.

A person can become ready to let go of their problematic traits even if they do not believe in a traditional God. In fact, some might argue, all anyone can do is become ready and ask for help, as is suggested in Step 7. Even if one is a "do-it-yourself-er," the process of becoming ready to make a change is still important. I use the Zipper Line activity to allow participants an opportunity to publically state their intention of bringing about a positive change in their behavior. Group Scrabble also offers a clever way to think about giving up "characters," or letters, that are no longer useful.

STEP 6 ACTIVITIES

Zipper Line

Materials Needed: One pool noodle for each group member. If you don't have pool noodles, extended arms can easily be used instead.

Approximate Time: 5 minutes

Description: Zipper Line is a trust-building activity in which one person at a time says the phrase "I'm ready to let go of _____," filling in the last word with a character defect of their choice such as envy, self-downing, pride, self-righteousness, etc. Ask your group members to form two lines facing each other so that each person is facing someone in the opposing line, about three feet away. Pool noodles or arms should be extended to create a zipper effect between the two lines where the opposing arms or noodles overlap. Then, one at a time, group members stand at the front of the "zipper line" and announce whether they will walk, jog, or run through the line as the human drawbridge opens just in time to clear an open path for them passing though. If a person ducks as they pass through, I usually invite them to repeat the process, this time standing tall as they move through the line.

Processing Points: What did it feel like to become ready to let go of a problematic behavior? What might be possible for your group members if they actually could become free of whatever holds them back? Also, what issues came up for people as they moved through the line? Did their damaged sense of trust from former relationships impair their ability to trust the group?

Group Scrabble

Materials Needed: A "team-building" Scrabble set. The letters of a traditional Scrabble set should be replicated using materials that can be seen from a distance. You can cut a pool noodle into narrow slices for this purpose or use old tennis balls. Most tennis facilities acquire many used tennis balls, so with a small amount of effort you can build a team Scrabble set for free!

Approximate Time: 15–20 minutes

Description: One definition of "character" is a letter in the alphabet. I use Group Scrabble (also described in chapter 8) as a way for people to get rid of

"I'm ready to let go of _____." *Photo by Dennison Webb*.

their defects of "character," or letters, that are no longer working for them. You can keep the small groups that were formed in Commonalities, but this activity works best in groups of five to seven.

Just as in the board game, each member draws a letter from the pile of tennis balls or pool-noodle slices that each have a letter written on them. Each small group is challenged to come up with a five- or six-letter word that then must be displayed so that people in other groups can read it, with each group member holding one letter. Team members can exchange non-useful "characters" for newer, more helpful ones by discarding the unwanted "character" in the pile of letters and taking a new one. I then ask the group to say their word out loud in unison. You can add a stipulation that the spelled words must have some connection to recovery. After each group has formed a word, increase the letter count for the following round.

These warm-up rounds can be followed by a full game of Group Scrabble in which all of the letters are eventually used to create a large crossword puzzle on the floor.

Processing Points: What roles emerged as the two teams worked to form words? Were the roles individual team members played functional or problematic? Did they reflect the roles they take on in other contexts? Some people have a tendency to seize control while others tend to fade into the background. Offer an opportunity to talk about these dynamics, both during the game and in the broader world.

STEP 7 ACTIVITIES

Humbly asked Him to remove our shortcomings.

Human Knot

Materials Needed: One bandana or pool noodle for each group member
Approximate Time: 10 minutes
Description: Human Knot is a classic problem-solving activity in which group members become "knotted" together and then attempt to untangle the knot without letting go of the object that is being used to connect them (in this case, a folded bandana or a pool noodle). Using props instead of hands or wrists to connect people allows group members to engage in the activity without being distracted by the discomfort associated with prolonged hand-holding. If using pool noodles, a character defect can be written on a strip of tape attached to each noodle.

Group members are asked to stand in a circle and extend their right hand holding a bandana or pool noodle. Then each person is instructed to grasp someone else's bandana or noodle, but it can't be the same person who has grabbed theirs, and it can't be the person to their immediate right or left. The

Collectively untangling a mess. *Photo by Ben Silverman.*

challenge is then for the "human knot" to become untangled without anyone letting go of their connectors. The knot comes to represent the group's collective defects of character, and God works through the collective energy of the group to "remove" the defects by untangling the knot. In this sense God is represented by the group-as-a-whole, which functions as a "higher power" in that it is a power greater than any one individual group member.

There are several potential outcomes to the group's efforts. Most often, the group is successful at becoming untangled without anyone having to let go. Sometimes, two separate circles emerge from the knot, and once in a while the group reaches an impasse whereby one minor adjustment needs to be made in order for the group to complete the task. This is much like life itself: sometimes we need to make minor modifications of our original plan in order to be successful. This kind of flexibility is a good alternative to the perfectionism that plagues many.

Processing Points: If character defects are written on the noodles, allow your group members to read what was written on them. I prefer to have each person read a character defect other than the one they wrote down. That way the group is emphasized over individual voices, and people have an opportunity to see that they are not alone with the challenge of personal growth.

This activity offers an opportunity to explore the boundary between personal responsibility and trusting in one's higher power. The wording of the seventh step suggests an absolution of responsibility for one's behavior, yet the task involves willingness *and effort* on behalf of the group members. "Humbly asked Him to remove our shortcomings" suggests that willingness is enough. This activity makes it clear that effort is required in addition to willingness. How does this idea function when working the seventh step? For example, if I ask God to remove my procrastination, that may not be enough to get the job done. I may also have to stick to a schedule, make "To do" lists, and build some accountability by sharing my goals with someone else.

Finally, conceptualizing the collective character defects of the group can facilitate a discussion about personal boundaries. Do we have a tendency to take on others' problematic behaviors and make them our own?

STEPS 8 AND 9

Made a list of all persons we had harmed, and became willing to make amends to them all. Made direct amends to such people wherever possible, except when to do so would injure them or others.

Steps 8 and 9 are the least amenable of all the steps to team-building activities, but I have found some creative ways to work with both steps, presented below. Step 9, being an interpersonal step, is amenable to traditional group therapy formats such as discussion and psychodrama, and a straightforward discussion can be a welcome interlude in an ABC program after the activities of the first eight steps. Psychodrama is a good technique for Step 9 because, like the other activities in this book, it is an active and highly structured way of working, providing energy and excitement for the group members. In working with Steps 8 and 9, a healthy level of trust between therapist, patients, and the rest of the group must be in place because of the high level of personal vulnerability involved in these steps.

STEP 8 ACTIVITY

Tarp Turn

Materials Needed: One 6×8-foot plastic tarp, two rolls of masking tape, and some markers

Approximate Time: 10 minutes

Description: Ask your group members to write the initials of someone they have hurt through their addiction on a piece of tape. Place the tape strips on one side of a plastic tarp. Flip the tarp over, tape-side down, and ask your group members to stand on the tarp. The strips of tape represent the group's collective Step 8 list, and the process of flipping the tarp (described in chapter 13)—as in the metaphor "turning over a new leaf"—represents the group's willingness to make amends to those they have hurt.

Processing Points: Especially when working with people newer to recovery, even *thinking about* Steps 8 and 9 can be daunting. It may be enough to pose the question "If you were to make amends to someone you have hurt, who would be at the top of your list and why?" This discussion can be used to evoke Step 8, Step 9, or both.

STEP 9 ACTIVITY

The Empty Chair

Materials Needed: All you really need is a chair for every group member plus two extra chairs set up in front of the group. These chairs define the "stage" on which the psychodrama will be developed. It can be helpful to have an assortment of props and costume pieces available for people to work with. For example, you might have some caps of various types on hand, a tie, scarves in a variety of colors, other accessories, and some household items. Such props and pieces of clothing can enhance the impact of the psychodrama, but they are not required.

Approximate Time: 30 minutes to one hour or longer

Description: Techniques of psychodrama can be used to help group members rehearse their amends-making. Psychodrama, developed in the mid-20th century by Jacob L. Moreno, borrows elements from the theater to help bring group members' stories to life. Moreno was a traditionally trained psychoanalyst who felt that his patients would benefit from more active methods. Rather than simply letting patients rehash their narratives through talking, psychodrama offers patients an opportunity to viscerally experience dramas from their lives and, most importantly, develop an ability to see difficult situations from another person's point of view. In fact, role reversal, the psychodramatic technique in which an individual role-plays an antagonistic person in their life, may be psychodrama's most powerful contribution to psychotherapy.

With group members seated in a semicircle, ask them to think about the person whose initials they wrote down during Tarp Turn or another person to whom they would be willing to make amends. One helpful feature of psychodrama is its versatility. The method can be used to make amends even when making amends in real life is impossible. It can also be used to examine and correct amends that did not work out as one had hoped. A rehearsal through psychodrama can also be used to address and work through feelings of guilt and remorse, on the one hand, and residual anger on the other, which might otherwise contaminate the amends-making process.

The two chairs are set up in front of the horseshoe of other chairs. These two chairs should be angled slightly toward the audience, while remaining opposite each other so as to facilitate face-to-face conversation. A group member is invited up to the "stage" to tell their story. That person is called the "protagonist" for this exercise. Ask the protagonist to choose someone from the group to sit opposite them to play the receiver of the amends. That person, called the "auxiliary," is directed to sit opposite the protagonist in the second chair in front and to simply listen to the amends.

Role-reversal techniques can be used to give the protagonist an opportunity to respond *as the other person*. The protagonist is directed to stand up, exchange places with the auxiliary, and when seated in the auxiliary's chair, the protagonist is positioned to become the recipient of the same amends. The auxiliary now repeats the protagonist's amends in the same spirit and words, as closely as possible, as the spirit and words of the protagonist. Remember, we want to illuminate *the protagonist's* story, so it's important that the auxiliary player doesn't impose their own story on the one being played out. The protagonist, now in the role of the receiver, can be directed to respond. Another role reversal and a final response completes the conversation. To illustrate, I provide a case vignette.

> After having given the group members an opportunity to reflect on those whom they have harmed during their active addiction, the group leader provides a cursory explanation of psychodrama. A group member responds to the invitation to tell his story to the group. We'll call him Brad. Brad sits in one of the two chairs at the front of the room.
>
> Therapist: Okay, Brad, can you tell us what happened? What's the story?
>
> Brad: I did a lot of crazy shit during my addiction, and a lot of people got hurt in the process. I have spent a lot of time thinking about this one dude who I shot in the knee. It was a drug deal gone bad. I was driving and my buddy was in the back seat with this other dude.
>
> Therapist: Can we give your buddy and the other dude names?
>
> Brad: The dude's name was James. My buddy was Mike.
>
> Therapist: Okay, go on.
>
> Brad: So, anyhow, I was driving and James was in the back seat with my buddy. So, all of a sudden, this dude James pulls out a gun as I'm driving, and he starts pointing it in my buddy's direction. I freaked out and I didn't know what to do, so I just grabbed this pistol I had in the car door and shot a couple of shots back in the dude's direction. One of them hit the back of the seat and the other one hit him in the knee. Then my buddy pushed the dude out of the car while the car was moving. I never did find out what happened to that guy. I don't know if he's alive or dead.
>
> Therapist: Can we bring James up here? Who would you like to play James? (Brad indicates another group member, whom we'll call Bill.) Bill, are you willing? (Bill indicates that he is, and he takes the seat opposite Brad.) Now, Brad, go ahead and make the amends to James. He is right here in front of you.
>
> Brad: Hey, man, those were some crazy days back then. We were all doing some crazy shit. I kind of freaked out and just didn't know what to do. I had to try to protect

myself and my buddy, and that's why I took a shot at you. I'm sorry I hurt you and I'm sorry we pushed you out of the car. I really hope you were able to recover and I just want you to know that I am truly sorry for what I did. I would never be in that situation now.

Therapist: Okay, now please switch chairs with each other. Bill, you are now Brad. And Brad, you are now James. Brad (the therapist is saying this to Bill), I'd like you to make the amends to James, as closely as possible to the way you just heard Brad say the words.

Bill (as Brad): Hey man, those were some crazy days back then. None of us knew what we were doing. I really didn't want to shoot you, and I just didn't know what to do. I kind of panicked. I just want you to know that I am truly sorry that I shot you and then that my buddy pushed you out of the car. I sincerely hope that you were able to recover, and I really am sorry.

Therapist (to Brad): James, what do you want to say in response?

Brad (as James): I think I had it coming to me, man. I had no business pulling a gun on you guys. Anyhow, I made it through. I spent a few days in the hospital, but I got put back together. Anyway, I appreciate what you're saying.

Therapist: Reverse roles again, so switch back to your original seats, and we will go through the whole thing a third time. Brad, start at the top, by making the amends, then (to Bill) you, James, will respond, just as you heard the response a minute ago, and Brad will have an opportunity to respond to you. Okay, go ahead.

Brad: Hey, man, those were some crazy days back then. We were all doing some crazy shit. I just didn't know what to do. I had to protect myself and my buddy, and that's why I took a shot at you. I'm really sorry I hurt you and I'm sorry we pushed you out of the car. I really hope you were able to recover. I just want you to know that I am truly sorry for what I did.

Bill (as James): I think I had it coming to me. I should not have pulled a gun on you guys. I did make it through. I spent a few days in the hospital, but I got put back together. I appreciate what you're saying.

Therapist (to Brad): How do you want to respond?

Brad: That's good to know, man. I'm glad you got put back together, and most of all, I am glad you survived. I've been feeling guilty as hell about what happened, so it's good to know that you survived and that you're okay now.

Therapist: Good. Can you talk about what feelings are coming up in you as you go through this process?

Brad: I feel relieved. I haven't been able to stop thinking about that dude and wondering what ever happened to him.

Therapist: Okay, let's take some time for sharing now. (The therapist checks in with other group members.) Can others relate to feelings of guilt and remorse and obsessing about what might have happened to people who were in our lives at one point? Each of you take a turn and share one incident from your own experience that relates to Brad's work.

Other group members now have an opportunity to talk about what came up for them as the psychodrama was played out. After everyone has had a chance to share, go through the process of "de-roling," as follows:

Therapist: Okay, we're going to de-role now. Brad, I need you to say, "I am Brad, I am not James."

Brad: I am Brad, I am not James.

Therapist: Bill, can you stand up and say, "I am Bill. I am not Brad and I am not James."

Bill: I am Bill. I am not Brad or James.

Therapist: Thank you both. You can return to your seats in the semicircle. Who else would like a chance to be the protagonist?

As mentioned previously, psychodrama is flexible. The vignette can be replayed to represent how the protagonist *wishes* their amends might be received, as in the illustration above. It can also be used to ventilate feelings that were repressed during an actual attempt at amends-making. In more advanced groups, participants in the audience can "double" for the protagonist, especially a protagonist less articulate than Brad, by standing behind them during the psychodrama and echoing or paraphrasing what's being said or putting into words what's not being said about the situation. For example, a group member might have doubled for Brad during the above vignette, saying, "When I saw the gun, I thought, 'Holy Shit!' I became terrified." Or another member might double, saying, "I was enraged and shot my gun in anger, and only later I realized I had been really scared." This is a great way to clarify and even enrich the experience of the protagonist as well as the group, involving more group members and making the endeavor a group project, while creating a shared understanding within the group. For a more thorough explanation of psychodrama, please refer to Dayton (2005) and Yablonsky (1976).

Processing Points: There will inevitably be much to discuss with respect to Steps 8 and 9. Please be aware that transitioning from games and team-building challenges to psychodrama has a tendency to quickly change the group's mood from playful to somber, and this may take some group members by surprise. Discussing scarred relationships can be far more threatening than the physical trust-building activities they did during Steps 3 and 5 earlier in the day. It's important to give group members permission to participate in the psychodrama at whatever level they feel ready to. If the group is reticent and no one wants to come up to take a turn as the protagonist, the therapist can direct the group to divide into pairs. Each person in a pair can take a turn as the protagonist, telling a story of when they had done harm to someone. The protagonist is directed to rehearse making amends while the other group member plays the role of the recipient. Each pair is directed to proceed, as described above.

Note that during the "sharing" portion of the psychodrama, the protagonist learns they are not alone in their experience as everyone has had similar experiences. The sharing of stories fosters empathy between group members and significantly enhances the cohesion of the group as a whole. Be sure to allow enough time for everyone to relate their feelings and associations with the protagonist's work before moving on.

STEP 10

*Continued to take personal inventory and
when we were wrong promptly admitted it.*

The tenth step offers an opportunity for immediate application. If you are facilitating an ABC program for people in treatment, allow a few minutes for reflection on how the day has unfolded so far. Is there anything that your group members might do differently if they could rewind the day and start over? What "wrongs" are they aware of having committed during the day? You can use the principles embedded in this step to process any activity, but Fireball below lends itself particularly well to self-reflection.

STEP 10 ACTIVITIES

Over-Under-Through

Materials Needed: Two long bungee cords or similar material and two structures to anchor them to. These can be two trees if outdoors or two long tables turned on their narrow ends when inside.

Approximate Time: 15 minutes

Description: Over-Under-Through, sometimes referred to as Electric Fence, offers an opportunity for group members to be rigorously honest with themselves and others—a core tenet of recovery. The two bungee cords should be stretched between the two support structures with one at knee height and the other at approximately waist height. The group is challenged to get all of its members from one side to the other *without making contact with either cord.* This means that one third of the group members will crawl under the low cord, a third will climb over the high cord, and the last third will pass through the two cords. Those going through and over will benefit from the visual and physical support of their group members. Let your group members know that if anyone touches a cord, that person will start over. For a tougher challenge, say that the whole group will begin again if anyone (note that this includes both support people and those crossing) touches the cords.

Processing Points: This activity offers an opportunity to talk about integrity. Is it up to the facilitator to judge whether or not participants have made contact with the cords, or is this something group members can do for themselves? This relates closely to long-term recovery. After urine tests and breathalyzers are things of the past, it becomes incumbent on each individual to monitor their own sobriety.

Practicing rigorous honesty. *Photo by the author.*

Fireball

Materials Needed: A rubber ball that is easy to catch and throw
Approximate Time: 10 minutes
Description: Fireball, also described in chapter 7, begins as a simple ball-tossing activity. It evolves into an opportunity for group members to reflect on their judgments of themselves and each other, and it also provides an opportunity for group members to increase their integrity, a key tenet of recovery from addiction that is particularly relevant to Step 10.

Ask a group of eight to 15 group members to stand in a circle and begin passing a ball back and forth between them using only their non-dominant hand. You can begin with a Name Game such as Group Juggling if a refresher would be helpful. After group members have become comfortable tossing and catrching the ball or object, announce that you will now introduce some new criteria. Ask that group members take a step back from the circle if they feel that they have made a bad toss, made a poor catch, made any extraneous noise, or made any extraneous movement. You can start with the first two of these and then introduce the other two criteria one at a time or start with all four at once. Stop the round when there are a few people left. If it is taking too long for people to make an error and step back, make the circle a little bigger or speed up the play. For the next round, keep the same criteria but say, "This time, step out of the circle if you make a bad throw or catch, if you make any extraneous noise or movements, *or* if you judge someone else as having made a poor catch or throw." This invites group members to reflect on ways in which they judge others as well as themselves. Again, stop the round when there are just a few people left. For the final round, keep all the previously established criteria but add that if you, the facilitator, point at a group member, that person should also step back from the circle. This offers an opportunity for group members to experience the difference between taking action based on self-determination versus being told by others what to do.

Processing Points: This activity is highly transferable to other settings, and it can lead to some very rich processing. Anecdotally, it seems as if about half of those who enter recovery do so of their own volition, while the other half do so only at the urging or insistence of a loved one or other authority figure. Ultimately, if recovery is going to stick, the recovering person needs to own the decision to stay sober. People in early recovery may be actively wrestling with this decision, especially if they initially entered treatment based on someone else's advice. The final round of Fireball offers a nice metaphor for this crucial notion.

You might also want to discuss what it felt like for people to toss the ball using their non-dominant hand. How was the experience of trying out a new behavior during this activity similar to or different from learning to live a sober life?

Source: Straus, 2016.

STEP 11

Sought through prayer and meditation to improve our conscious contact with God, as we understood Him, praying only for knowledge of His will for us and the power to carry that out.

Like Steps 8 and 9, Step 11 does not easily lend itself to interactive challenges. Prayer and meditation are usually, though not always, solitary pursuits. Roth (2004) makes a case for group therapy offering an opportunity for prayer and meditation whereby listening to others in the group functions as a kind of meditation, and talking to the group can be seen as a form of prayer. I give myself license to use guided meditation, body scan relaxation, or the ubiquitous Serenity Prayer. However, Zen Counting below does offer a sense of collective meditation or listening without judgment.

STEP 11 ACTIVITY

Zen Counting

Materials Needed: None
Approximate Time: 5 minutes
Description: Ask your group members to spread out randomly and, with their eyes closed, count aloud from 1 to 20 without two people saying any given number in unison. If this occurs, the group starts over again until it is successful. This activity functions as a group meditation.

Processing Points: Sometimes doing less is the most helpful thing we can do toward helping a group accomplish its goal. When else is doing nothing the most helpful (non-) action we can take?

STEP 12

Having had a spiritual awakening as the result of these steps, we tried to carry this message to alcoholics, and to practice these principles in all our affairs.

This step lends itself very well to kinesthetic activities. Really, any task that connects everyone in the group through a progression of behavior will work as a metaphor for Step 12. There are many such examples, and I offer a few of my favorites below.

STEP 12 ACTIVITIES

Marble Pass (aka Channels)

Materials Needed: One piece of half-pipe per group member (the half-pipe can be made from a length of PVC tubing cut in half lengthwise), a marble, and a container
Approximate Time: 10 minutes
Description: This classic team-building activity offers an apt metaphor for "carrying the message," whereby the marble becomes a collective message of recovery (e.g., serenity, determination, honesty, etc.). You can invite your group members to assign a quality of recovery to the marble. With each group member holding a small half-pipe, the group members stand side by side and attempt to pass the marble via each individual half-pipe from point A to point B and then to deposit it into a container that represents others who are ready to hear the message of recovery. This activity can be effective for fostering good communication and acceptance among the group members. If the marble falls during the attempt, ask the group to start over from the

beginning. This can add an element of frustration for some group members, which is good practice for the stressors of "carrying the message" of recovery.

Processing Points: People are often quick to place blame when things go wrong. When the marble drops to the ground, what feelings arose for participants? When else in life are we eager to attribute blame? When a family member is struggling with underperformance or a mood disorder, do relatives attribute blame or do they look for ways to support their loved one? The same questions can be applied to group members' experience during Marble Pass.

Stepping Stones (aka River Crossing)

Materials Needed: One portable platform, or "stepping stone," for each group member. These can be made from pieces of foam, carpet samples, slices of a tree trunk, spot markers, or, as a last resort, pieces of paper, and they should be large enough for one to two people to stand on at the same time. I have also used small foam kickboards for this purpose. You'll need as well some way to mark the "banks" of the river.

Approximate Time: 15 minutes

Description: Stepping Stones is another classic team-building activity in which the group is challenged to get from point A to point B by stepping only on identified "stepping stones." Each person is given a stepping stone and is asked to endow it with an aspect of recovery that they really rely on. The group must then use these recovery tools to get safely across the "River of Temptation" that has been designated by the facilitator. If any group member falls into the river (i.e., steps onto anything other than the stones), the group needs to start over. Also, it is important that group members stay physically connected to their resources. If at any time a resource is sitting in the river and not being touched, stepped on, or stood on by a group member, it will be lost (in other words, the facilitator will take it away). Staying connected to one another tends to help the group stay stable and be successful during this activity. See the description of this activity in chapter 13 for more detail and an image of Stepping Stones.

Processing Points: In what ways do your group members stay connected to others in recovery? If they try to go it alone, are they more vulnerable to relapse? What impedes people's willingness to reach out for help on a continual basis? Also, what prevents your participants from using their resources on a consistent basis? If they "let go of their resources," say by no longer meeting with their sponsor or going to meetings, are they putting themselves at risk?

Source: Gass, 1995.

Carrying the message. *Photo courtesy of Lance Eagen.*

Instant Impulse

Materials Needed: None
Approximate Time: 2 minutes

Description: This is a "quickie" for Step 12. Ask all the group members to stand in a circle, holding hands. The group leader squeezes the person's hand to his or her right, who passes the impulse in turn to the person to their right by gently squeezing that person's hand, and so on until the energy returns to you, the group leader. Then pass another impulse to the left. How about both at once? Since people are joining hands and standing in a circle, this is a nice time to end with the Serenity Prayer.

Processing Points: I always end RAD with some time for reflection on and a review of the overall experience. What "message" did participants take in during the day? Time permitting, I ask group members to share one thing that they will take away from the experience and apply to their recovery going forward. Often people will remember the importance of asking for and accepting help as this theme is stressed throughout RAD. Others will have been impacted most by their role and tendency to either consistently seize control of the group or consistently withhold themselves from the group. An epiphany regarding their valence for a particular role in groups can be a valuable lesson. Finally, some group members will emphasize that they were able to engage freely in play while remaining sober.

Give Yourself a Hand

Materials Needed: An assortment of small plastic hands that can be attached to a keychain, available online from Training Wheels or as part of the RAD kit, also available from Training Wheels (see appendix)

Approximate Time: About one minute per group member

Description: Your participants deserve a hand for all the hard work they did with you and to remind them that they became physically engaged in their recovery during their time with you, so it might be a good idea to offer participants small plastic hands to commemorate their experience. This little memento reminds participants that long-term recovery will be dependent on their dedicating their heads, their hearts, and their hands to the process much as they did during the program. Give each participant an opportunity to "give themselves a hand" by stating something they did during the day that they feel good about. Group members can support each other in this process by stating the laudable qualities they saw in each other during the day. After each individual mentions a personal strength that got expressed during RAD, allow them to select a plastic hand of their choice. Having the hand on their keychain may serve as a reminder that a helping hand is always available if it is sought.

Note: While all of the activities described in this chapter are portable and can be done in a large group room, if you happen to have access to an outdoor challenge course, there are many additional activities that can function as metaphors for the recovery process. For example, Whale Watch, in

Adventure wall—mutual support in action. *Photo by the author.*

which group members try to balance the group on a giant seesaw, can function as a metaphor for finding balance in life between work and recreation or action and rest.

Many other outdoor challenge course activities can function as living enactments of the Steps. Challenges such as The Wall, Nitro Crossing, Adventure Walk (see the figure), and Spider's Web can represent Step 2, for example. Each of these challenges requires that participants use the support of the group (which functions as a higher power in the parlance of the 12 Steps), and in so doing they may "come to believe" that they can attain a sober life by using whatever support is available.

High ropes courses are ideal for embodying Step 3 as participants really are, at least temporarily, "turning their will and lives over" to the care of a higher power—in this case, the facilitators, the designers and builders of the course, and in some instances, their fellow group members.

Additionally, high ropes challenges are exhilarating and may provide the adrenaline rush that some sought through their addictive behavior. As I've noted, people who are predisposed to addiction have a higher tolerance for stimulation than most people (Cain, 2012). Traveling along a zipline or traversing a wire suspended 30 feet off the ground is a safe way to meet these

Having faith in the group's support. *Photo by the author.*

needs. Finding ways to have sober fun is the key to successful recovery, and the activities described here and in the preceding chapters may help recovering individuals realize that having sober fun is a goal well within reach.

Appendix

Resources

The following are some good places to access training and materials for facilitating ABC activities.

Adventure Forward Therapy

Founded by Barney Straus, Adventure Forward Therapy provides therapeutic adventure-oriented retreats as well as training for therapists interested in using ABC. Barney specializes in programing to support recovery from addiction. You can learn more at www.adventureforwardtherapy.com.

The Association for Experiential Education (AEE)

AEE is a global community of experiential educators and practitioners with the shared goal of enriching lives through experiential education. The Therapeutic Adventure Professional Group within AEE offers training specifically geared to therapeutic populations. See www.aee.org.

FUNdoing

Directed by Dr. Chris Cavert, FUNdoing promotes pro-social education and the development of emotional intelligence through adventure education activity programming. Chris has written many books on adventure education and he offers a free bimonthly email filled with team-building activity resources. You can sign up for the email at www.fundoing.com.

High 5 Adventure Learning Center

Based in southern Vermont, High 5 Adventure Learning Center is a nonprofit educational organization dedicated to helping individuals, teams, schools, communities, and businesses improve the way they live, learn, and work together. You can learn more at www.high5adventure.org.

Project Adventure

Project Adventure is committed to promoting adventure and experiential education as a catalyst for positive and lasting growth. To that end, they seek to deliver exemplary training, programs, publications, and challenge courses that inspire those transformations. You can learn more at www.pa.org.

Sensorimotor Psychotherapy Institute

Based in Los Angeles, the Sensorimotor Psychotherapy Institute offers training internationally and in different parts of the United States. Further information can be found on their website, www.sensorimotorpsychotherapy.org.

Training Wheels

Training Wheels is a provider of adventure programming training and materials. Director Michelle Cummings offers an array of props as well as individualized training for facilitators and groups. She offers a free weekly newsletter as well. The Recovery Adventure Day Kit can be ordered from Training Wheels. You can access all of this at www.training-wheels.com.

References

Aguire, B. (2013). *Mindfulness for borderline personality disorder: Relieve your suffering using the core skills of dialectical behavior therapy.* Oakland, CA: New Harbinger Publications.

Alcoholics Anonymous. (1999/1952). *Twelve steps and twelve traditions.* New York: Alcoholics Anonymous World Services.

———. (2001/1939). *Alcoholics Anonymous: The story of how many thousands of men and women have recovered from alcoholism* (4th ed.). New York: Alcoholics Anonymous World Service.

American Psychiatric Association. (2013). *Diagnostic statistical manual of mental disorders* (5th ed.). Washington, DC: American Psychiatric Association.

Aristotle (1961). *Poetics,* translation by S. H. Butcher. New York: Hall and Wong.

Asprey, D. (2017). *Head strong: The bulletproof plan to activate untapped brain energy to work smarter and think faster—In just two weeks.* New York: HarperCollins.

Black, C. (1981). *It will never happen to me.* New York: Random House.

Blech, J. (2009). *Healing through exercise: Scientifically-proven ways to prevent and overcome illness and lengthen your life.* New York: Rodale.

Brooks, D. (2018). The power of human touch. *New York Times.* January 19, A25.

Brown, S. (2010). *Play: How it shapes the brain, opens the imagination, and invigorates the soul.* New York: Avery.

Cain, J., & Jolliff, B. (1998). *Teamwork and team play.* Dubuque, IA: Kendall Hunt.

Cain, J., & Smith, T. (2002). *The book on raccoon circles.* Tulsa, OK: Learning Unlimited.

Cain, S. (2012). *Quiet: The power of introverts in a word that won't stop talking.* New York: Random House.

Cavert, C. (2015). *Portable teambuilding activities: Games, initiatives, and team challenges for any space.* Bethany, OK: Wood 'N' Barnes.

Cavert, C., & Sikes, S. (1997). *50 ways to use your noodle: Loads of land games with foam noodle toys.* Tulsa, OK: Learning Unlimited.

Cavert, C., Sikes, S. (2002). *50 more ways to use your noodle: Loads of land and water games with foam noodle toys.* Tulsa, OK: Learning Unlimited.

Cavert, C., & Thompson, B. (2017). *Cup it up! Team building with cups.* Barry W. Thompson.

Comer, E., & Hirayama, K. (2009). Activity: Use and selection. In A. Gitterman and R. Salmon (Eds.), *Encyclopedia of social work with groups.* New York: Routledge, 117–18.

Cummings, M. (2007). *Playing with a full deck: 52 team activities using a deck of cards!* Dubuque, IA: Kendall Hunt.

Cytrynbaum, S. (2014). *Summary of group relations assumptions, structural and psychological assumptions.* Handout for Group and Organizational Dynamics Graduate Seminar, Northwestern University, Evanston, Illinois.

Dayton, T. (2005). *The living stage: A step-by-step guide to psychodrama, sociometry, and experiential group therapy.* Deerfield Beach, FL: Health Communications.

Dayton, T. (2007). *Emotional sobriety: From relationship trauma to resilience and balance.* Deerfield Beach, FL: Health Communications.

Dayton, T. (2010). *The living stage: A step-by-step guide to psychodrama and experiential group therapy.* Deerfield Beach, FL: Health Communications.

Dewey, J. (1938). *Experience & education.* New York: Simon & Schuster.

Diodge, N. (2015). *The brain's way of healing: Remarkable discoveries and recoveries from the frontiers of neuroplasticity.* New York: Viking.

Dokoupal, T. (2012). Is the web driving us crazy? *Newsweek* , July 9.

Duhigg, C. (2012). *The power of habit: Why we do what we do in life and in business.* New York: Random House.

Eckert, L. (1998). *If anybody asks me . . . 1001 questions for educators, counselors, and therapists* . Bethany, OK: Wood 'N' Barnes.

Eig, A. (2017). Using rough and tumble play in group psychotherapy. *International Journal of Group Psychotherapy, 67*(3), 40–32.

Ellis, A. (1996). *Better, deeper, and more enduring brief therapy: The rational emotive behavior therapy approach* . New York: Brunner/Mazel.

Faulkner, S. (2002). Low-elements ropes course as an intervention tool with alcohol/other drug dependent adults: A case study. *Alcoholism Treatment Quarterly, 20*(2), 83–89.

Fletcher, A. (2013). *Inside rehab: The surprising truth about addiction treatment and how to get help that works.* New York: Viking.

Flores, P. (2004). *Addiction as an attachment disorder.* Boulder, CO: Jason Aronson.

———. (2006). Conflict and repair in addiction treatment: An attachment disorder perspective. *Journal of Groups in Addiction & Recovery, 1*(1), 5–26.

Forbes, B. (2011). *Yoga for emotional balance: Simple practices to help relieve anxiety and depression* . Boston, MA: Shambhala Press.

Freimuth, M. (2005). *Hidden addictions.* Lantham, MD: Jason Aronson.

Gardner, H. (2011). *Frames of mind: The theory of multiple intelligences.* New York: Basic Books.

Garland, J., Jones, H. E., & Kolodny, R. (1965). A model for stages of development in social work groups. In S. Bernstein (ed.), *Exploration in Group Work.* Boston: Charles River

Gass, M. (1995). *Book of metaphors, Volume II.* Dubuque, IA: Kendall Hunt.

Gass, M., & Dobkin, C. (1988). *Book of metaphors: A descriptive presentation of metaphors for adventure activities* . Dubuque, IA: Kendall Hunt.

Gass, M., Gillis, H. L., & Russell, K. (2012). *Adventure therapy: Theory, research, practice.* New York: Routledge.

Gass, M., & McPhee, P. J. (1990). Emerging for recovery: A descriptive analysis of adventure therapy for substance abuse. *Journal of Experiential Education, 13*(2), 29–35.

Goldstein, B. (2018). Working beneath the words: Group therapy through the lens of sensorimotor psychotherapy. American Group Psychotherapy Society Annual Meeting, Houston, Texas.

Goldstein, B., & Siegel, D. (2013). The mindful group: Using mind-body-brain interactions in group therapy to foster resilience and integration. In D. J. Siegel & M. Solomon (Eds.), *Healing moments in psychotherapy.* New York: W. W. Norton.

Hagedorn, W. B., & Hirshorn, M. A. (2009). When talking won't work: Implementing experiential group activities with addicted clients. *Journal for Specialists in Group Work, 34*(1), 43–67.

Hammond, D., & Cavert, C. (2003). *The empty bag: Non-stop, no-prop adventure-based activities for community building.* FUNdoing Publications.

Hayden, C., & Molenkamp, R. (2004). Tavistock primer II. In S. Cytrynbaum & D. A. Noumair (eds.), *Group Relations Reader 3.* Jupiter, FL: AK Rice Institute.

Horne, L. (1997). The twelve steps experientially. In *Deeply rooted, branching out, 1972–1997*, Annual AEE International Conference Proceedings.

Itan, C. (Ed.). (1998). *Exploring the boundaries of adventure therapy: International perspectives*. Boulder, CO: Association for Experiential Education.

Kirby, M. (2016). *An introduction to equine assisted psychotherapy: Principles, theory, and practice of the Equine Assisted Psychotherapy Institute model*. Australia: Balboa Press.

Korshak, S., & Delboy, S. (2013). Complementary modalities: Twelve-step programs and group psychotherapy for addiction treatment. *Eastern Journal of Group Psychotherapy, 37*(4), 273–94.

Korshak, S. J., Nickow, M., & Straus, B. (2014). *A group therapist's guide to process addictions*. New York: American Group Psychotherapy Association.

Kurland, R., & Salmon, R. (1992). Group work vs. casework in a group: Principles and implications for teaching and practice. *Social Work with Groups, 15*(4), 3–14.

Le Fevre, D. (2002). *Best new games*. Champaign, IL: Human Kinetics.

Levine, P. (2010). *In an unspoken voice: How the body releases trauma and restores goodness*. Berkeley, CA: North Atlantic Books.

Lung, M., Stauffer, G., & Alverez, T. (2008). *Power of one: Using adventure and experiential activities in one on one counseling sessions*. Bethany, OK: Wood 'N' Barnes.

Luscombe, B. (2016). Porn-induced erective dysfunction: Is it a virility threat? *Time*. March 30.

MacKinnon, A. (1998). *Using adventure methodologies in residential drug treatment*. Self-published.

Maguire, R., & Priest, S. (1994). Treatment of bulimia nervosa through adventure therapy. *Journal of Experiential Education, 17*(2), 44–48.

McCormick, R., & Ortez, C. (2014). *Umbuntu activity guide*. Brattleboro, VT: High 5 Adventure Learning Center.

Mellody, P. (1989). *Facing codependency*. San Francisco: Harper & Row.

Metzl, J. (2013). *The exercise cure: A doctor's all-natural, no-pill prescription for better health & longer Life*. New York: Rodale.

Middleman, R. (1980). *The non-verbal method in working with groups: The use of activity in teaching, counseling, and therapy*. Hebron, CT: Practitioners' Press.

Norton, C. L., Tucker, A., Russell, K. C., Bettmann, J. E., Gass, M., Gillis, H. L., & Behrens, E. (2014). Adventure therapy with youth. *Journal of Experiential Education, 37*(1), 46–59.

O'Donnell, M. (2014). High ropes courses in adventure therapy: Supplemental intervention for substance abuse treatment. Research proposal for SOWK 606, Research Methods, Loyola University Chicago School of Social Work, Chicago, Illinois.

Ogden, P. (2018). The role of the body in group psychotherapy: A sensorimotor psychotherapy approach. American Group Psychotherapy Society Annual Meeting, Houston, Texas.

Ogden, P., & Goldstein, B. (2018). The role of the body in group psychotherapy: A sensorimotor psychotherapy approach. American Group Psychotherapy Association Annual Meeting keynote address, Houston, TX.

Popkin, B. (2009). *The world is fat: The fads, trends, policies, and products that are fattening the human race*. New York: Avery Press.

Quereau, T., & Zimmermann, T. (1992). *The new game plan for recovery: Rediscovering the positive power of play*. New York: Ballantine Books.

Ringer, M., & Gáspár, J. (2017). *Experiencing outdoor spaces and places from within: Adventure therapy and systems psychoanalysis*, 34th ISPSO Annual Symposium, Copenhagen, 2017.

Rohnke, K. (1984). *Silver bullets: A guide to initiative problems, adventure games, and trust activities*. Dubuque, IA: Kendall Hunt.

Rohnke, K., & Butler, S. (1995). *Quicksilver: Adventure games, initiative problems, trust activities, and a guide to effective leadership*. Project Adventure.

Rohnke, K., & Grout, J. (1998). *Back pocket adventure*. Needham Heights, MA: Simon & Schuster.

Roth, J. (2004). *Group psychotherapy and recovery from addiction: Carrying the message*. New York: Haworth Press.

Russell, K. (2003). A national survey of outdoor behavioral health programs for adolescents with problem behaviors. *Journal of Experiential Education, 25*(3), 322–31.

———. (2008). Adolescent substance-use treatment: Service delivery, research on effectiveness, and emerging treatment alternatives. *Journal of Groups in Addiction and Recovery, 2* (2–4), 68–96 .

Rutan, S., Stone, W., & Shay, J. (2007). *Psychodynamic group psychotherapy, 4th Edition .* New York: Guilford Press.

Sandberg, S. (2017). *Plan B: Facing adversity, building resilience, and finding joy.* New York: Random House.

Scheff, D. (2013). *Clean: Overcoming addiction and ending America's greatest tragedy.* Boston, MA: Houghton.

Schiller, L. Y. (1997). Rethinking the stages of development in women's groups: Implications for practice. *Journal of Social Work with Groups, 20*(3), 3–19.

Schoel, J., & Maizell, R. (2002) *Exploring islands of healing: New perspectives on adventure-based counseling.* Beverly, MA: Weston Walsh.

Schoel, J., Prouty, D., & Radcliffe, P. (1988). *Islands of healing: A guide to adventure-based counseling.* Hamilton, MA: Project Adventure.

Schwartz, D., Nickow, M., Arseneau, R., & Gisslow, M. (2015). A substance called food: Long-term psychodynamic group treatment for compulsive overeating. *International Journal of Group Psychotherapy, 65*(3), 387–410.

Short, E., & McRae, M. (2010). *Racial and cultural dynamics on group and organizational life: Crossing boundaries.* Los Angeles: Sage Publications.

Sikes, S. (2003). *Raptor and other team-building activities.* Liberty Hill, TX: Doing Works.

———. (1998). *Executive marbles and other team-building activities,* Tulsa, OK: Learning Unlimited.

Simpson, S., Miller, D., & Bocher, B. (2006). *The processing pinnacle: An educator's guide to better processing.* Oklahoma City, OK: Wood 'N' Barnes.

Spolin, V. (1983). *Improvisation for the theater.* Evanston, IL: Northwestern University Press.

Stagnitti, K., & Cooper, R. (Eds.). (2009). *Play as therapy: Assessment and therapeutic interventions.* London: Jessica Kingsley.

Straus, B. (2008). Zoom. In S. S. Fehr (Ed.), *101 interventions for group therapy.* New York: Haworth Press.

———. (2013). New hope discovered during recovery adventure day. *New Hope Treatment Center Newsletter.*

———. (2016). Fireball. In S. S. Fehr (Ed.), *101 interventions for group therapy, second edition.* New York: Routledge.

Sussman, S., Lisha, N., & Griffiths, M. (2011). Prevalence of the addictions: A problem of the majority or minority? *Evaluation & the Health Professions, 34* (3) , 3–55.

Van der Kolk, B. (2014). *The body keeps the score: Brain, mind, and body the healing of Trauma.* New York: Viking Press.

Wasson, S. (2017). *Improv nation: How we made a great American art.* Boston, MA: Houghton, Mifflin, Harcourt.

Weiss, R., Jaffee, W., de Menil, V., & Cogley, C. (2004). Group therapy for substance use disorders: What do we know? *Harvard Review of Psychiatry* (November/December).

Williams, F. (2017). *The nature fix: Why nature makes us happier, healthier, and more creative.* New York: W. W. Norton.

Wright, W. (2005). The use of purpose in ongoing activity groups: A framework for maximizing the therapeutic impact. *Social Work with Groups, 28*(3/4), 205–27.

Yablansky, L. (1976). *Psychodrama: Resolving emotional problems through role-playing.* New York: Basic Books.

Yalom, I. D. (1995). *The theory and practice of group psychotherapy* (4th ed.). New York: Basic Books.

Yalom, I. D., & Leszcz, M. (2005). *The theory and practice of group psychotherapy* (5th ed.). New York: Basic Books.

Index

activities, sequencing of, 35–36
addiction: prevalence of, 143; treatment of, 144
Adventure-Based Counseling (ABC), vii; and boundaries, 14–15; definition of, xiii–xiv; as exercise, 13; history of, xv–xvii; and long-term group therapy, xvii; materials used in, 31–32; and recovery from addiction, 143–191; therapist's role in, 29–31; training for, 30–31; for trauma survivors, 13–21. *See also* trauma
Adventure Forward Therapy, 193
Adventure Therapy, xvii; definition of, xiii
adventure wave, 36
Alcoholics Anonymous (AA), 3, 8, 145, 147, 148; 12 steps of, 45, 153–191
The Association for Experiential Education, xii, 31, 193

Cavert, Chris, xi, xii, 45, 105, 113. *See also* FUNdoing
challenge course, xvii
Cognitive Behavioral Therapy (CBT), vii, xviii, 26–28, 36, 144; and treatment planning goals, 28
Cummings, Michelle, 99, 194. *See also* Training Wheels

Dewey, John, xvii

Dialectical Behavior Therapy (DBT), vii, 26, 28
Diodge, Norman, 14. *See also* neuroplasticity
Duhigg, Charles, 143, 145

Flores, Phil, 144–145
Freud, Sigmund, xiii
FUNdoing, 193. *See also* Cavert, Chris

Gass, Michael, xii, xiii, 4–5, 23, 143, 145, 154
Goldstein, Bonnie, xviii, 15, 16, 120
groups: as a whole, 3; definition of, 3; stages of development of, 6; therapeutic factors of, 7–12

habit formation, 143. *See also* Duhigg, Charles
Hahn, Kurt, xvi. *See also* Outward Bound
Hammond, Dick, 113
High 5 Adventure Learning Center, 194

intensive outpatient programs (IOP), vii, viii, xiv, 6, 12, 28–29
Itan, Christian, 146

Kurtz, Ron, 120

Leszcz, Molyn, viii, 6; and therapeutic factors of groups, 7–12, 54 metaphor: neuroplasticity, 14; therapeutic use of, 4–5, 8

nature, therapeutic value of, 23–24

Ogden, Pat, 31, 96, 120, 121
Outward Bound: philosophy of, xvi; therapeutic value of, xiv–xv

partial hospitalization programs (PHP), viii, 6, 28–29
perceived risk, 18–21
Pieh, Jerry, xvi–xvii. *See also* Project Adventure
play: stages of, 24–26; therapeutic value of, xiii, xvi
Project Adventure, xvi, 194
psychodrama, 180–183

Recovery Adventure Day, 149–191; kit, 32, 194
recovery from addiction, 143–191; 12-step programs and, 148
Rohnke, Karl, xii, xv
Roth, Jeffrey, 14, 145, 169, 186

Russell, Keith, 144

Sensorimotor Psychotherapy Institute, 120, 194
Sikes, Sam, 45, 131
Straus, Barney, xiv–xv, 145

Teachers of Experiential and Adventure Modalities (TEAM) Conference, xv
Thompson, Barry, 105
touch, therapeutic use of, 16
Training Wheels, 194. *See also* Cummings, Michelle
trauma, 13–21

umbuntu, 8

van der Kolk, Basel, 13, 13–14, 15, 21, 26, 27

Yalom, Irvin, viii, 6; and therapeutic factors of groups, 7–12, 54

About the Author

Barney Straus, LCSW, CGP, is a psychotherapist in private practice with Working Sobriety in Chicago. He is the founder of Adventure Forward Therapy, a practice dedicated to using adventure-based methods to help clients achieve their therapeutic goals. In addition to providing group and individual therapy, Barney offers adventure-based retreats and trainings. He is also a part-time faculty member at Loyola University Chicago's School of Social Work and Roosevelt University's Department of Psychology. Barney is a certified group psychotherapist and a fellow of the American Group Psychotherapy Association.

Barney has presented numerous workshops at national and international conferences on using adventure activities with therapeutic populations. He has developed a special adventure therapy program called Recovery Adventure Day (RAD), which is specifically designed to support people in recovery from addiction.

Barney has had articles and book reviews published in the *Journal of Groups in Addiction and Recovery* and the *International Journal of Group Psychotherapy*. He is coauthor of a manual on treating process addictions with group therapy that was published by the American Group Psychotherapy Association.

www.ingramcontent.com/pod-product-compliance
Lightning Source LLC
Chambersburg PA
CBHW021816270326
41932CB00007B/204